P9-DUA-527

Seeds of Disquiet

Seeds of Disquiet

One Deaf Woman's Experience

Cheryl M. Heppner

Gallaudet University Press
Washington, D.C.

Gallaudet University Press
Washington, DC 20002

© 1992 by Gallaudet University. All rights reserved

Published 1992

Printed in the United States of America

Library of Congress Cataloging in Publication Data

Heppner, Cheryl M., 1951–
    Seeds of disquiet : one deaf woman's experience / Cheryl M.
Heppner.
      p. cm.
    ISBN 1-56368-016-5 : 17.95
    1. Heppner, Cheryl M., 1951– . 2. Deaf—United States—
Biography. 3. Women, Deaf—United States—Biography. I. Title.
HV2534.H43A3   1992
362.4'2'092—dc20
[B]   92-9693
                                       CIP

For Fred, with whom I've fallen in love five times by the last count. Your patience, good humor, caring, and ability to have fun got me through this book just like they did everything else.

For Rosemary Green, Ron Heath, Tootie Campbell Rinker, Angie Papke, LaRita Jacobs, Gay Nagy, Fred Yates, Joan Cassidy, and Linda Miller, for sharing with me, pushing me, and allowing me to keep growing.

For Mom and Dad: this isn't the trip around the world, but a glimpse inside mine. I hope the journey is as rewarding and that your confidence in me will be repaid.

For Randy, who helped me make the great leap of faith, and for Gayle and David—a good family to rally around.

And for the many friends who shaped my thinking, whose names are engraved in my mind forever, although they do not appear in this book.

Prologue

In July 1989, I went to Washington, D.C. to attend the Deaf Way conference. It was the first international conference on Deaf culture. I had spent a week sharing experiences with persons from all over the world. Deafness was our common thread. It was exciting to be part of a conference with so many thought-provoking speakers. I had one more workshop to attend, then I'd head home to sift through what I had learned.

In the lounge of the hotel restroom, I added a layer of lipstick to the remains of an earlier one. Eyes wandering from my mirrored reflection, I scanned my surroundings. Another woman was seated in a softly-lit corner, dabbing at red-rimmed eyes.

I turned, concerned. "Are you all right?" I asked. Unsure whether she was deaf or hearing, I signed my question as I voiced it.

"I'm fine," the woman signed back. But a fresh flood of tears coursed down her cheeks.

I faced the mirror again, unconvinced but wanting to respect her privacy. Then I felt myself drawn back.

Four steps brought me to the woman. "No, you're not all right," I told her. Kneeling, I hugged her with all the strength and kindness remembered from other people, other hugs.

We talked for a few minutes, minutes that sped us across lifespans, transcending everything. She was from Michigan. Her hearing, never perfect, had begun to deteriorate during the past few years. As she'd tried to adjust to the loss, her marriage to a hearing man had ended. She'd met a deaf man who offered her acceptance and caring. She was beginning to hope that happiness was within reach. But her life was changing rapidly, and the changes frightened her. She wanted desperately to share her fears with someone who would understand.

I was that person. So much of what she said had happened to me. I listened and gave what comfort I could from the patchwork of my experiences. In those moments we created our own private, intense global-warming trend. Two friends had found each other.

Then we were separated in a mad rush of bodies as people crowded the hotel hallway. I never knew her name. She left my life as abruptly as she entered, leaving feelings that would not go away. Two weeks later, I began to write this book.

I have met so many people who became deaf and struggled to understand their feelings! Not so long ago, I was one of them, and often, still, I am a seeker too.

Deafness changed my life at the age of six and forced me to begin a long struggle for respect and understanding. I've read books by the bagful about deafness, many of them written with great sensitivity by parents, family members, and professionals. But we who are deaf have only recently begun to talk about many of the things that trouble us.

Writing this book was by far the hardest work I've done. As I flipped the Rolodex in my brain, searching for words that would express my thoughts, two sides of me traded punches.

One side wanted to pull out the memories of anger, fear, and shame for reappraisal. The other side fought to keep them hidden. It was a well-matched contest at first, but the memory-puller side won.

Slowly, I peeled back the layers of my life and looked where I had buried what hurt me most. "When you look long into an abyss, the abyss also looks into you," Friedrich Nietzsche once said. Over and over, that phrase came into my thoughts. Writing this book forced me to stare into the abyss and face my demons.

Those unforgettable moments with my anonymous friend pushed me to start this book. Nancy Kingsley gave me the incentive to finish it.

After eighteen months of writing and rewriting, my words were on paper, and I had stared down plenty of demons. But I wasn't ready to put my feelings on public display. I stored my work carefully in the drawer of my desk and busied myself writing short pieces. I did articles about closed captioning and battery recycling programs for several publications. For these, words came easily.

Then I got a letter from Nancy. Nine years before, she'd read an article about me, written by Julie Dunlap, who worked for the Associated Press. Julie was an old college friend who had spent several days with me, focusing on my struggles to adapt to hearing loss and on my activist's lifestyle. Her article had found its way into newspapers across the country, including the one Nancy subscribed to.

"At the time I read the newspaper clipping about you, I had not yet been able to come to terms with my disability," Nancy wrote me. She said the article helped her realize that we had much in common. She had since experienced a radical change in attitude about herself and her life.

These many years later, she'd read my article about the importance of recycling and reusing hearing aid batteries. She was shocked to realize that the author of the article was the same woman profiled in the yellowed clipping she had saved. She immediately wrote to tell me of my influence on her life.

Two women reached out to remind me of the importance of sharing. They credit me with giving them strength. I hope this book will help them realize that I took as much as I gave, if not more. Their struggle for answers has inspired me and will never be forgotten.

1

I was the second child born to parents who had both been eldest children. My ancestors were of hardy stock, and my extended family is close and boisterous on one side, scholarly and intense on the other.

My mother was raised in Waterville, Maine. Her father, Gramp Webber, operated a dairy farm on land that had nourished his wife's family, the Goodwins, for generations. The lush, gently curving fields were grazed by cows that had only passing interest in small girls but were extremely mindful of the movements of Gramp's collie.

Gramp Webber stood well over six feet in height and was an imposing figure even in his field clothes. Although he was a man of few words, I never feared him. When he sat down to rest at the end of a long day, the tenderness with which he stroked his loyal collie's broad head clearly showed his gentle nature.

Gram Webber was a stoic. She, too, was spare with her words, and her blunt statements were made with total conviction. She took the bounty from the fields, of which corn and strawberries were my favorites, and turned them into meals that I always ate too much of. Her flaky biscuits and her lemon-banana ice cream, which she froze in ice cube trays, were tastes

I lived for. Gram was a typical country cook; she used no recipe books. Every ingredient in her dishes was measured by some variation of a pinch or a handful.

My great-grandmother Goodwin also lived on the farm. She had deep lines on her face from years of being warmed by the sun, and her back had curved in a perpetual stoop. Each morning she gathered her white hair in a bun and went to work without fanfare. Gram Goodwin was never far from the gardens she loved. I watched her bend to pick peas or weed beets and marveled at the sureness and economy of her movements. I always thought of her whenever I read the poem mounted on Gram Webber's kitchen wall:

> *The kiss of the sun for pardon,*
> *the song of the birds for mirth—*
> *One is nearer God's heart in a garden*
> *than anywhere else on earth*

While most of the farmland had been cleared, magnificent old trees still sheltered the big white farmhouse and lined the lazily-flowing roads. Beyond the fields I had a view of the glorious Kennebec River, often cluttered with logs heading downstream to the pulp mills.

At the edge of the farm, a cluster of tall pines ringed the family graveyard. I was fascinated by the size of the grave mounds, and I stretched out on some of the larger ones to get the full measure of their length. I had a suspicion that Paul Bunyan's offspring had married into the Goodwin family.

Gram Webber was fond of wild birds. She had several feeders to entice them, despite their eagerness to pillage her blackberry and raspberry bushes. Gramp had built a flagstone terrace behind the house, with a stone fireplace and a roof to protect the terrace from rainstorms. Gram had added a large white picnic table, benches, and lounge chairs, and we often took our meals there. The air was sweet with the scent of lilac and lily of the valley, which grew in profusion nearby.

My father's parents, the McIntoshes, lived in a solid brick house in Lisbon Falls, a couple of hours south of Waterville. They were both natives of the area. Gramp was short and powerfully built. Gram didn't clear five feet in height, and I never knew her to have a waist.

Gramp McIntosh liked to dabble at farming. He grew only a few salad vegetables. Cucumbers and radishes seemed to be the limit of his interest. He quickly taught me to appreciate their cool crunch on a hot summer day. He also grew a nice crop of rhubarb next to the house. I loved the taste of rhubarb stewed with sugar to blunt its tartness.

Soon after I was born, Gram and Gramp moved to a house closer to the post office and next to the Episcopal Church they attended. Gramp McIntosh was the town postmaster, but he also played many other roles. He was a politician, a real estate agent, a church elder, a member of the Masonic lodge, and an eager eater with the Lobster Club. His feet and his friends got him everywhere; he never drove a car.

Walking with Gramp was always an event. He greeted everyone he saw by name, and treated them all as if they were his buddies. He would stop to talk with people whether they were dressed in frills or in rags. Gramp lived frugally, but he was extremely generous to others. More than once, when he thought no one one was looking, I saw him slip a few dollars into the pockets of people everyone called "bums."

Gram McIntosh had been a piano player for silent movies. She played the organ at church on occasion, and could be coaxed into volunteering her musical skills for special events. She was tremendously loving and fiercely protective. Her children and grandchildren could do no wrong; she loved us all without reservation. When she hugged me to her ample, rose-scented bosom, I believed that nothing in the world could touch me.

Dad's two brothers were quite a bit younger than he was, and at the time I was born, they still lived with Gram and

Gramp. They were like night and day. Bruce, the shy one, was preparing for college. Terry was hamming his way through high school.

Many of my aunts and uncles had gravitated toward the teaching profession, but my parents hadn't felt the same pull to become educators. They met in a business college and married after Dad returned from Navy service in World War II. Mom left her job as a medical secretary to have children. The Worumbo Mill, one of Lisbon Falls's major employers, claimed Dad. This woolen mill was located at the edge of the town on the bank of the Androscoggin River.

My older sister Gayle was the first grandchild for both sides of the family. With only two years' difference in our ages, Gayle and I were close, though you'd never have guessed from our constant bickering.

Dad and Mom built a comfortable Cape Cod house about a mile away from Dad's parents' home. Gayle and I shared a large bedroom with a walk-in closet so big that it doubled as a playroom.

I loved our house and I loved the neighborhood. We lived next door to my godparents, Evelyn and Oliver Woodhouse, whom we called Auntie Ev and Uncle Ollie. They had two children. Peter was born within a month of Gayle, and John beat me into the world by less than three weeks. In the stretch of yard between our houses, we learned to play croquet, badminton, and many other games.

Gayle and I loved to visit Gram and Gramp Mac. In their yard, they had a tiny white house that became our playhouse. Gram and Gramp kept it stocked with decks of cards and our favorite games: Chutes and Ladders, Candy Land, and Go to the Head of the Class. Adults rarely bothered us while we played with our friends and cousins in the Little House.

Uncle Terry made a great babysitter for me and Gayle. He had all kinds of strange games. One night he kept us occupied by throwing a deck of playing cards onto the floor and timing how fast we could pick them up. He was also a witness for the first of my many scrapes on wheels, when I learned that riding a tricycle full speed while wearing my mother's dresses was hazardous. I caught the hem of a dress beneath the wheels. When the thrust pulled me over the handlebars, I left part of my cheek on the concrete floor.

I picked blueberries in the nearby woods and watched pollywogs sprout legs in the brook behind our house. Most of the neighborhood kids my age were boys who weren't too keen on any activity involving dolls. They taught me to eat apples green and tart off the tree, sprinkled with salt for an extra kick. And they showed me how to get the best bang when hitting rolls of red caps with a rock. I rode the neighborhood with them after Dad took the training wheels off my secondhand bike.

Gayle and I were fans of the Loony Tunes, the Mickey Mouse Club, Robin Hood, Howdy Doody, Romper Room, and Captain Kangaroo, which we watched regularly on our black and white television. For a special treat, Gram Mac would take us to see the newest Disney cartoon features at the theater. We also belonged to a Brownie troop for which Mom served as an assistant.

My favorite place in the world was Old Orchard Beach, where the Woodhouses had a summer cottage. I loved to build sand castles, collect snails, and find interesting shells. I routinely frightened my parents because I had no fear of the water. Before I learned to swim, I liked to dive. If I saw a good wave roll in, I'd take a deep breath, dive beneath it, and wait for my parents to scoop me out of the water as I was swept toward the shore.

On lazy days at the beach, Dad and Uncle Oliver helped me, Gayle, Peter, and John fly kites and burn designs in driftwood with a magnifying glass. At night, we often walked to the pier, which had a magnificent old carousel with wooden horses. We were happy exploring the fun houses, riding the ferris wheel, or bashing each other with the bumper cars.

We ate a specific Beach Cuisine, maybe because the dishes were the only ones two families of picky eaters could agree on. Mom and Auntie Ev made lots of submarine sandwiches and American or Chinese chop suey. We were fond of "devil dogs" and made many trips to nearby Saco for box lunches of fried clams and french fries topped with a warm dill pickle.

I was an average child in every way, if somewhat more trying due to three personality traits—independence, stubbornness, and unending inquisitiveness. Peter Woodhouse gave me the nickname "Punky" because he claimed that I wasn't afraid of anything. I sometimes overheard relatives compare me unfavorably with Gayle, who, by all accounts, unfairly bypassed much of the "terrible twos."

For a while I had a great scam going. After receiving an apron as a gift, I wore it at every meal. My folks thought I was getting maximum enjoyment from it. What they didn't know was that I took mixed vegetables and other food I disliked from my plate and hid the stuff in the pockets of my apron. When the food got cold and began to soak through the fabric, I'd ask to be excused from the table. My explanation that I needed to visit the bathroom was true. That was where I flushed the food down the toilet. My deception was eventually discovered after my mother decided to wash the apron before I had had a chance to empty the pockets.

When I was five years old, I walked to school with Gayle for the first time. Mom and Dad bought us new saddle shoes for the occasion. My name was a popular one the year I was born—my class also had a Cheryl White and a Cheryl Black. In the Lisbon Falls schools I made the amazing discovery that both crayons and library paste had interesting flavors. It's amazing that I lived to adulthood.

Mrs. Jones, my first grade teacher, guided me expeditiously through the beginning readers. I zipped from *We Come and Go* to *Fun with Dick and Jane* and then *Our New Friends.* In the meantime, I came down with a series of illnesses—chicken pox, measles, colds, flu—and, finally, just as I started second grade, spinal meningitis.

2

At first the family doctor thought my sickness was one of the flu viruses making the rounds in the community. But when my temperature continued to shoot up and I started to hallucinate, he knew I was grappling with something more serious. It was an anxious time for my family, but there were pleasant moments for me. As my body lay in bed, I felt weightless, and I imagined myself floating above my room, watching everything that happened with fascination.

I was out of school for nearly four months while recovering, from November 1958 until February 1959. Twice I was admitted to Massachusetts General Hospital in Boston, where I had tests, spinal taps, and consultations. My mother stayed with her sister Marilyn and came to see me during visiting hours. She tried to keep me occupied with books and toys.

I hated the hospital. It was frightening to be in a strange place and not be able to understand what was being done to me. The boredom, the lack of exercise, the endless poking and probing by a succession of strange people, and the fear at being separated from my family made me very anxious.

Doctors discovered that I had a permanent, profound hearing loss. Whatever feelings my parents had about the news, they either hid or could not share with me. They busied themselves with the task at hand—trying to cope with a child who had been suddenly deafened.

Oliver and Evelyn Woodhouse were all smiles when they came to visit me during my recuperation at home. There were days I could barely move, and I was sometimes in pain, but Uncle Ollie would pick me up effortlessly in his burly arms. He and Auntie Ev amused me and took my mind off the aches and unrelenting boredom.

Many years later, my mother confided that one of her great sorrows was knowing that I would never again hear music. On one of our visits to Mass General, she heard Christmas music being played. When she saw that I was totally oblivious to the carols I had loved, she was devastated. She left the room so that I would not see her tears.

I had been surrounded by music since the day I was born. My family didn't have the trendiest of clothes or the neighborhood's best landscaping, but there were always funds to spare for the current hit records. The years before I lost my hearing were bathed in the many moods created by music. I was a loyal fan of the Mickey Mouse Club and my favorite singer was Rosemary Clooney.

Gayle and I had planned to follow in Gram McIntosh's footsteps, and we had been taking piano lessons. It was at the piano that I first began to notice the fading of my hearing. The keys became hollow-sounding and disembodied, as if I were playing the piano from a great distance.

My parents had been told by several doctors that I should be sent to a school for the deaf in Portland, Maine. A social worker, however, gave them conflicting advice. Mom and Dad still remember his words clearly. "Raise her as normally as possible," he said. "If she goes to the deaf school in Portland she will be out of the real world."

Choosing to follow the social worker's advice was a decision strongly reinforced after my mother met a recent graduate of the school for the deaf. He was twelve years my senior, but we were reading at almost the same level. My parents had no faith in a school that had been able to teach him so little.

The school system in Lisbon Falls agreed to send someone to work with me at home so that I could stay with my original class. My second grade teacher, Mrs. Demjanovich, graded me "Satisfactory" in all categories on my report card that year, just as Mrs. Jones had. But in those days, grades weren't given for subjects—they were for social objectives like school attitude, promptness, sportsmanship, and taking criticism profitably. Clearly I was turning into a good "comrade."

Deafness had made me something of a lost soul. Overnight, without hearing to reinforce it, my speech became all but unintelligible. And I couldn't automatically learn speechreading, so I was cut off totally from my friends, family, and teachers. The social worker at Mass General had told my parents not to allow communication by writing. He felt that I'd develop speaking and speechreading skills faster if I was forced to focus on them.

People would try to talk to me and then stalk away in frustration, with stormy looks on their faces. I was so wrapped up in my own troubles that I didn't realize these people weren't necessarily angry with me. I thought I had done some terrible thing to annoy them. I remembered that in the past I'd often heard people say I was not as well-behaved as my sister, and I began to believe that I was somehow doomed to be a bad person forever.

Everything had suddenly become *my* problem. And I associated all my problems with deafness. It seemed that my hearing loss had turned me into a very bad child indeed.

Going back to the classroom was difficult because everything confused me. I was also thoroughly embarrassed because my classmates liked to talk about the last time they'd seen me. Before I left school to recuperate from meningitis, I had become sick and lost my breakfast while seated at my desk. The kids liked to embellish the event. They told me about how vile the classroom had smelled, and how the teacher had thrown out my puke-covered books. They pantomimed the janitor coming to clean up the mess. Their stories weren't the kind of welcome I'd hoped for.

I was baffled by visits to fit me with hearing aids. In different offices I saw several shiny boxes connected to cords with an earpiece at the end. Over and over I was asked to listen and tell which shiny box sounded the best. I didn't know what I was supposed to listen for; I heard nothing remotely like the sound I was used to. I became so fed up with the testing that I decided to insist on a Zenith, just to be done with it. I wore my new hearing aid in a shirt pocket or in a cloth harness across my chest.

My parents were able to find a speech therapist thirty miles away in Augusta. She could only work with me for a half hour every week, so I made little progress in learning to speak or speechread.

I survived much of that rough transition to deafness by developing an active fantasy life. A stuffed toy dog became my superhero partner-in-crime, a Mighty Mutt who could fly, stop speeding bullets, and drink pink Kool-Aid by the pitcher. I shut myself inside the walk-in closet and spent hours as a princess in my make-believe world.

The summer after I lost my hearing, my father was asked by Woolrich Woolen Mills to come and interview for a job. The mill was a small, historic, family-run business tucked in the mountains of central Pennsylvania. Years later, I found out that Dad hadn't been interested in the position until officials at the mill told him about a speech therapist in the area who was willing to work with me, both in school and at home. That incentive proved so great that he accepted the job sight unseen.

Moving away from Maine, where my aunts and uncles were rapidly providing interesting new cousins, was a wrench.

I was leaving the land of ever-loyal, ever-frustrated Red Sox fans. More important, I was losing my close contact with Gram McIntosh, who had been hard of hearing for years. She was the one person with whom I felt a special empathy. I was also very attached to the Woodhouses, in whose home and beach house I had played as often as in my own home.

I was dreadfully unhappy and fearful of the move. My year had been one of tremendous upheaval. Throughout all the changes in my life, I'd at least had the stability of a home and friends and plenty of relatives nearby who had known me before I became deaf. Suddenly those were being taken from me.

We arrived in Woolrich on August 5, 1959, just in time to celebrate my father's birthday. The town seemed to be a classic rural community. One main street branched at the center of the village and returned to wind its solitary way north. There was one park, one pool, one post office (located in the one store), one school, one factory, one church—and suddenly, one deaf child.

I missed my friends in Maine, especially John Woodhouse, whom I'd planned to marry in ten or twelve years. In fact, I missed just about everything. There were no blueberries in the Pennsylvania woods behind my new home, and no ponds full of pollywogs. I was far from the wind-swept seacoast with its wild beaches and stiff, cleansing winds.

3

I was eight years old when I showed up in Woolrich School's third-grade classroom. I had been in town for almost a month, but I hadn't met many of my classmates. Most of them came by bus; some were from remote areas.

My new school was small and stable. It had only one class for each grade. There were twenty-seven kids in my third-grade room, and most of the other grades were the same size. Only a few families moved in or out of the area each year, so I was more than the usual oddity.

My teacher, Mrs. MacKenzie, made me feel welcome and tried to smooth my entrance to her class. I was beginning to be desperate for friends and anxious for some routine in my life. I was still trying to adjust to sounds that didn't make sense while being surrounded by new faces and returning each afternoon to a house I wasn't used to.

The stress level increased when I discovered that I couldn't read any writing on the blackboard. Arrangements were quickly made to take me for vision tests, and I was fitted for eyeglasses. I hated my glasses because they always seemed to fly off when I was playing baseball or freeze tag.

Mrs. MacKenzie was alert to my progress. When she saw that I couldn't grasp the multiplication tables my classmates were studying, she notified my mother. Mom was ripe to become Mother Martyr of the Year. She took me aside when I arrived home and started to drill me on the tables. I tried everything in my repertoire to get out of those drills over the next few days, but neither tears nor screams budged her resolve. She was going to drum those tables into me if it killed her, and she looked plenty tough enough to live to a ripe old age.

I quickly learned to multiply, but I also learned something else. I never wanted to endure my mother's drills again. I watched my classmates carefully and made sure Mrs. MacKenzie wouldn't be making any more calls.

The Cold War was on and the Red Menace was in high hysteria. I lined up with the other students at Woolrich School for regular bomb drills. But most of the time, I was being nurtured by wonderful teachers, and I flourished under their attention. Midway through the year, Anna Belle Emerick took over third grade from Mrs. MacKenzie, and she stayed to become my fourth-grade teacher. Mrs. Emerick had lost some of her hearing, and my fifth-grade teacher, John Randecker, had limited use of one arm. Their experiences with disabilities must have given them insight into the struggles of a confused deaf child. They were marvelous teachers.

After Mrs. Emerick's arrival, my grades improved, and during elementary school I never again was graded "average" or below in any class, save a lone "C" for the first quarter in sixth-grade geography.

The school principal and sixth-grade teacher, John Barry, kept a stern demeanor to hide his marshmallow-soft heart. I was blessed several times in seeing him without his disciplinarian's mask, so I knew a gifted and gentle teacher that few other students did. Rounding out the team that taught me at Woolrich School was my speech therapist/tutor/super booster, Tom "Mr. Z" Zelinske, whose presence had persuaded my father to make the move.

Interpreters and assistive listening devices didn't arrive in time to help me get through school. But the confidence my teachers had in me inspired me to try things I didn't know I was capable of.

My teachers let me work at my own pace, and when I was unable to participate in class activities, they allowed me to read books. Every Saturday, my parents drove to nearby Lock Haven, where I checked out seven books, the maximum allowed, from the community library. I also borrowed books from the church library, but it was small and I quickly went through all the interesting titles.

I enjoyed reading so much that I would hurry to finish assignments so that I could bury myself in a book. I was keen on mysteries during fourth and fifth grade; I read every Agatha Christie and Erle Stanley Gardner book I could get my hands on. I knew Perry Mason, Miss Marple, and Hercule Poirot better than I knew my classmates.

My school day was, for the most part, one of independent study. On my fourth-grade report card, Mrs. Emerick noted during each grading period that I had a highly developed skill at "finding profitable things to do without being told." She certainly did everything to encourage it.

I was particularly fond of spelling competitions. If I couldn't speechread a word on my teacher's lips, my classmates would take turns trying to help me. Sometimes I'd find a classmate whose lips made a word become clear, or one who could pantomime the word in such a way that a light bulb went off in my head. I had an excellent visual memory; once I saw a word on a printed page, I could usually remember its spelling. Not being able to hear was probably an asset, since I wasn't tripped up by strange pronunciation before I could store a word in my brain.

I was beginning to enjoy writing. One of my poems was chosen as an entry in a contest. It was one the other kids could really relate to:

When I had chicken pox,
For many days of scratching
I thought I'd better live in a box
To keep my pox from catching.

During fifth grade, Mr. Randecker encouraged me to work on a science fair project. I had a lot of fun outfitting and labeling a terrarium to show how the water cycle worked. I was delighted when my project was chosen as the district winner.

There were some bad moments at Woolrich School, but rainbows often followed the storms. During fourth grade, my class started reading some of Beverly Cleary's Henry Huggins series. I had discovered the books earlier and fallen head over heels in love with offbeat characters like Ramona and Beezus. When my classmates started to take turns reading aloud for each other, I was anxious to share some of my favorite passages. I'd never taken part in that kind of activity, but Mrs. Emerick quickly granted my request to do so.

I stood in front of the class and read with all the enthusiasm I could muster. When I finished, I looked to my classmates, expecting to see them hanging on my every word. Instead, there were blank looks and yawns. I was so startled that my face contorted involuntarily. The classroom erupted with laughter. I was crushed. I had wanted to share a great story with them, and not only did they lack appreciation for my efforts but they were laughing at me!

For a half hour, I was inconsolable. Then Mrs. Emerick repaired the damage. She kindly sidestepped the fact that the kids were bored senseless because they couldn't understand my speech. Instead she wrote that they had not been laughing at me but at the funny face I'd made. The kids nodded their heads vigorously in agreement when she turned and asked them if it was true. Mrs. Emerick drew a cake on the blackboard, my reward for a good reading, and allowed me to choose from among my classmates to see who would have the honor of coloring it. After it was decorated, I was permitted to erase it, piece by piece, and "hand it out." What a roller coaster ride, from eager anticipation to depression to erasing an imaginary cake!

In fifth grade, heredity caught up with me. I was fitted with braces on my upper teeth and a retainer on my lower teeth. I felt like a robot. With my hearing aid, glasses, braces, and retainer, when I turned in any direction, something would glitter.

It was difficult to eat with all the wires in my mouth, so I usually took my retainer out before lunch. One day during sixth grade, I wrapped the retainer in a napkin and put it on my tray while I ate. When I finished lunch, without thinking, I dumped everything from my tray into the garbage can. An hour later, I suddenly realized what I had done. I confessed to Mr. Barry. He and Mr. Z went into the cafeteria, turned the trash can upside down, rolled up their sleeves, and unwrapped every napkin until they found the darn thing. It took a while. I had been one of the last to leave the cafeteria, so my trash had originally been on the top of the garbage can. Thereafter, Mr. Barry and Mr. Z loved to remind me of all the goo they'd gone through to save the day. I was thoroughly embarrassed, and even after Mom had soaked it in Lysol for a couple of days, I hated having that retainer back in my mouth.

4

Deafness was difficult for my classmates to grasp. They didn't understand that talking louder to me was no help at all. They didn't know why I needed to see their faces when they talked, or that they had to stand close to me so I could see their faces clearly. I was a demanding playmate compared to the others they could choose.

There was only so much we could do with a Barbie doll that didn't require talking. I gravitated naturally to sports and earned the reputation of being a tomboy.

At playtime I had two speeds, full throttle and dead stop. I was either playing something with enthusiasm or was lost in the worlds I read about in my books. Since I couldn't hear any side conversations, I played everything with single-minded intensity.

I liked to climb trees, walk in the woods with my dog, and play anything that didn't require hearing. I could play Red Light, even though it depended largely on sound, because kids always turned around when they shouted "red light!" All I had to do was watch them, and when their bodies started to move, I froze.

I eagerly joined Girl Scouts again. I couldn't get much out of many of the activities, but I had a blast working my way through the handbook. Collecting badges was one of my chief pastimes; I filled the front of one sash with them and started work on filling the back. It was easy to earn a badge by following the written instructions, doing a little research, and enlisting a generous parent for some of the requirements. I was good at self-directed learning.

My sister was as much a sports fan as I was, and we wanted very much to play Little League baseball. When we were turned down, we tried to start a girls' team. In our small town, by the time we had enough girls for a team, there weren't any left to play against. Once we persuaded the Little League team to play our ragtag, uncoached bunch, but we were soundly trounced.

Gayle and I spent a lot of our summer vacation at Woolrich Pool, which was operated by the woolen mill. Our entire family could use the pool for a reduced fee because Dad worked at the mill.

The pool was fed by a mountain spring, and it was a frigid tub of water when it was first filled in early June. During the morning, before the sun heated up, I often shivered my way through swimming and lifesaving lessons. After lunch, Gayle and I were back, waiting for the official opening at 1 p.m. We would stay until it was time for dinner and then come back until dark. The pool didn't have waves or the french fries garnished with vinegar and sand that we'd loved at Old Orchard Beach, but it was a great place to learn to stand on our hands underwater and dive off the springboard.

The woolen mill closed each year during the first week in July. We always packed into our station wagon and took off for Maine, where we split time between the two sets of grandparents. We could count on at least one good feast of lobsters and clams while Dad fulfilled his mission to recharge his accent.

Our biggest problem on the trip was Dad's obsession with getting places. Once he got in the car, Dad hated to stop for any reason. He'd usually allow one stop halfway to Maine, where we hit the restrooms while he gassed up the car. In between, we were told we'd have to use a peanut butter jar kept under the seat. Randy, who had problems with carsickness, was the only one who could persuade Dad to stop. There was nothing Dad hated more than the reek of vomit at close range.

Mom tried to make the trip bearable by planning all kinds of interesting food and games. It was one time of year that we bought comic books, which Gayle and I loved. We couldn't wait to get to Gram and Gramp McIntosh's, where we'd become reacquainted with our favorite things in the Little House and eagerly read the screen gossip magazines Gram left lying around. On Saturday night we had the traditional Down East meal of beans and franks. There were cukes and radishes at lunch and dinner, although Gramp sometimes brought them from the grocer instead of his garden. We commiserated about the latest difficulties faced by the Red Sox and speculated on the merits of their newest players. Before we left, Gramp always slipped a dollar or two into our pockets.

It was a McIntosh tradition to have some sort of family reunion on July 4th. Catching up with my cousins was tremendous fun, and so was eating too much food and watching the men try to outclass each other at horseshoes.

Mom and Auntie Ev continued to astonish the family by becoming pregnant at the same time. My brother Randy and Stephen Woodhouse were born within a month of each other, shortly before our move to Woolrich. Within two years, Dorrie Woodhouse made her appearance, followed within the month by my brother David. While we were on our Maine vacations, we always worked in at least one good day at Old Orchard Beach with the Woodhouse clan.

At Gram and Gramp Webber's farm, we hiked to the dam on the river. Gayle and I looked forward to visits from our cousins, Kathy and Kelly Stone. The four of us would imitate Gram's favorite television show—Lawrence Welk—by creating production numbers and blowing soap bubbles. I loved to sing, and I found an appreciative audience in the barn. I'd walk down the stalls where cows were being milked and belt out my favorites for their listening pleasure.

At home, my family was big on game playing. We loved new card games, especially weird and complex ones. We also played board games like Aggravation, Clue, Parcheesi, and checkers. I loved games like these because they were among the few things I could do with my family as an equal.

Nancy Hartman, who lived down the street, had toys galore and would sometimes invite me to visit. I liked being with her for the first three hours while I cased the joint. She didn't just have a doll, she had several—with wardrobes and a play kitchen to use for imaginary parties with her complete tea set. Unfortunately, after a couple of hours of showing me things, Nancy would want to start playing with them. Her lips barely moved when she talked, so I couldn't follow her fantasies. I became frustrated and anxious either to play by myself or go home.

Sharon Green wasn't the prettiest or smartest or best dressed kid in class, but she was nice to everyone, a trait that got her elected class president in sixth grade. I liked Sharon a lot, and when she told me that she sometimes walked to her aunt's house after school instead of taking a bus, I spied an opportunity. Her aunt lived near the old fire hall, Sharon said, and I remembered seeing a fire hall away from the direction of my house, down the street from the school. Sharon's friendship seemed well worth the sacrifice of a long walk.

I was excited to be building a relationship when I walked with her to her aunt's for the first time. She seemed hesitant, and I sensed that something was bothering her, but as usual she was unfailingly polite. As we neared the fire hall, I asked which house was her aunt's. It took some time to get everything straightened out, but I found out that I'd gone to the wrong fire house. Sharon's aunt actually lived near my house, and Sharon had been too polite to ask where I was headed. We stayed friends until we started high school, and I enjoyed our walks on many other occasions. When we tried to talk to each other, communication was very stilted, with many misunderstandings. But Sharon was such a good sport that I learned to overcome my frustration and enjoy just being with her.

In the later years of elementary school, boys and girls began to have separate activities at recess. I loathed the division of play according to sex because I wanted to be doing the boy stuff. I wasn't interested in the "let's pretend to be nurses and patients" games that the girls were playing, but I was no longer welcome in the boys' groups. Recess became an unhappy time for me.

The growing realization that boys and girls were different led to my first puppy love. In fifth grade, I fell for a freckled, red-haired boy. Just to be sure he knew how much I adored him, I wrote him a note headed "Why I Love You" and listed the reasons. He read the note, nodded kindly in my direction, and thereafter kept carefully out of my path.

My parents had resolved to raise me as normally as possible. They never tried to discourage me from doing anything that other children my age were doing. That included my dabbling in music, for which they must have suffered greatly.

The congregation of Woolrich Community Church was particularly indulgent, they allowed me to sing for years in the children's choir. I didn't think there was anything odd about it. I could memorize the words to songs and watch the choir director or the other children to be sure I was keeping up. However, I didn't understand what it meant to raise or lower the pitch of my voice or hold a key. My hearing aid made my voice appear to blend right in with the voices of other children. I didn't realize that the sound I heard was very different from what everyone else heard. On occasion, I sang quite lustily, whether the piece called for it or not.

In fourth grade, Woolrich School had a talent show. I watched the other kids strut their stuff and thought it would be neat to contribute something. So, on the spur of the moment, I asked if I could do a piano piece.

My teachers were astonished by my request, but they granted it. I hadn't had a piano lesson in the three years since I lost my hearing, but that didn't faze me a bit. I'd watched my sister practice. What's more, I'd seen the great pianists on television, and I knew how it was supposed to be done. My sister was but a peon in their shadow, and I intended to play like the giants. No "Home on the Range" or "Song of the Volga Boatman" for me.

I walked to the piano and seated myself with a flip of imaginary tails. Then I attacked the piano as I had seen pianists do, from Cliburn to Levant. I chose keys at random, depending on which interested me most, and changed rhythm whenever I felt like it. I was hot, and I knew it.

I finished with a flourish and turned to my audience. They stared in frozen silence; I thought they were too impressed with my brilliance to respond. One of the teachers lost her shell-shocked look and urged everyone to applaud. I was pleased.

No one ever had the heart to tell me that my performance stank, not even my poor sister, who sat through it with her friends from sixth grade. Time does wonderful things; now the talent show is one of her favorite stories.

An itinerant music teacher who came to my school gave me a clarinet to try. The first week I had it, I blew and blew, trying doggedly to find the secret to the magic vibrations. I'd look at a family member for approval, but headshakes told me that I was still producing nothing but wet, winded noises.

The second week, I hit pay dirt. I had the reed juiced to proper moistness and suddenly I felt vibrations so incredible that my lips became an engine. I was in heaven and ready to give Benny Goodman a run for his money.

Of course, the fact that I could make the clarinet vibrate didn't mean I could play it. My family's appreciation for my skill was nonexistent. It was no fun playing without encouragement, so I soon returned the clarinet to its owner.

I'd taken some dance lessons before I lost my hearing, so my folks thought tap dancing might be helpful to me. I wasn't keen on the classes, during which I tried halfheartedly to mimic the instructor. But practicing at home was a gas. The only spaces we had that were suitable for tapping were the concrete floor in the basement and the wood floor in the attic. The basement was cold and dim, and the concrete didn't carry vibrations. To everyone's dismay, I cleared a space in the attic and got the walls vibrating. I loved the volume and mass of the noise I could create, but my tapping clearly was not a favorite form of family entertainment.

Perhaps I was wrapped up in my fantasy life, which was much better than the world I had to cope with. Or maybe I was anxious over my place in the family after David was born and I had to compete with three other children for attention instead of two. Whatever the reason, I started to embellish on events and make them far more colorful. One day when I did particularly well in gym class, I went home and bragged that I'd performed truly amazing feats. After a field trip, I told my parents that I'd memorized the license plate of a speeding car and helped the police to nab the driver.

Mom and Dad must have known that I needed to feel important. They let me keep my fantasies and praised me for my imaginary exploits.

5

My elementary school years had three main focuses: school, my social life (or more often, nonlife), and my speech therapy sessions.

Tom Zelinske worked zealously on my speech. He was still a college student when he became my teacher. I memorized every detail of his face during the hours I spent watching it for speechreading information. His hair was so pale a blonde that it was almost white, and his eyes were a clear blue. The Miami Dolphins became one of my favorite football teams because coach Don Shula had a manner and body build that reminded me of Mr. Z.

Z's and s's were two of the hardest sounds for me to produce because my tongue and teeth refused to cooperate with each other. I took to calling Tom "Mr. Z" because it was hell to struggle through his full name.

I hated speech therapy, but I loved Mr. Z dearly and would do almost anything to please him. He had a marvelous bag of tricks and was quick to sense when my interest was waning. Much of speech therapy is pure, unending drudge work, but Mr. Z bent over backwards trying to make it, if not fun, at least bearable. When school was out for the summer, he'd work with me at home.

My mother was given the unhappy chore of reinforcing the work Mr. Z did with me at school. I loathed her practice sessions. Mom didn't have Mr. Z's flash cards and games, and she brought to her task the same drill sergeant's approach she had used to teach me multiplication tables. We were a touchy pair. I wanted to be outside playing like the other kids did after school. Watching my mother say boring things and then staring at myself in a mirror as I tried to copy the movements was no fun. I could match the lips, but the sounds coming from my mouth still wouldn't be right. To form words properly, I needed to know what happened in the mouth and throat, which were hidden from me.

For her part, Mom had other kids to keep out of mischief while she tried to work with me. She also had to prepare dinner, which the family expected promptly at 5 p.m. every day.

I resented my mother for putting me through the torture of those sessions and for one habit that always made me angry. When she wanted my attention, she'd put her hand under my chin and jerk my face around so that I had to look at her. I was too young to understand the concept of body space, but I certainly felt she was violating mine. The chin jerks made me feel hostile. I wasn't above closing my eyes and stubbornly refusing to watch her, which frequently earned me sound punishment.

Even though my communication skills were slow to develop, I was never encouraged to use writing to bridge the gap. I was expected to continue trying to speak until I was understood. When my family members spoke to me, they would repeat or rephrase their words to help me understand their speech. It wasn't a good system. There were three phrases I learned to hate above all others—"because I said so," "never mind," and "forget it."

Mr. Z was much more to me than a speech therapist. He also served as a tutor, encouraging me to test my limits. When I was a success, he praised me to the heavens; on the rare occasions when I had a setback, he was quick to offer sympathy.

During our sessions together at school, Mr. Z introduced me to subjects that my classmates would be studying in a year or two. Because I was ahead of my peers, Mr. Barry let me take some classes with the older students. By the time I entered high school, I was solidly prepared for many of the classes I'd be taking.

My sister is a sentimental person, and she loves any excuse for a party. When Gayle was in sixth grade, she found out that Mr. Barry's birthday was April 25, only four days before hers. She made sure I knew about it, since he would become my teacher in two years. I found out that Mr. Z was born on St. Patrick's Day, an easy date to remember.

I have never forgotten the love and caring these two men gave me. I still send them both birthday cards each year, a small gesture to let them know how much they've meant to me.

When I graduated from high school, Mr. Z wrote me his first and only letter, which I keep among my most precious possessions. In it, he shared for the first time his feelings for me, which were every bit as strong as mine for him.

In 1990, I was stunned to receive a letter from Mr. Barry, my first in twenty-eight years. He thanked me for remembering his birthday every year since 1962 and told me that it was a great honor to have me as a student and friend.

At the end of his letter, he wrote: "P.S., Remember not to lose your tooth retainer, if you have one."

6

In 1963, I started junior high school, riding the bus to Lock Haven for classes. There, I quickly began to lose the edge I had gained from the tutoring and extra attention I had received at Woolrich School.

I missed the closeness that came from having one teacher, small classes, and the same room all day. I no longer had the regular attention that Mr. Z had lavished on me. Still, there were some excellent teachers who went out of their way to be sure I kept up with my work, especially in seventh grade. My homeroom and math teacher, Mr. Abrams, and my English teacher, Mrs. Sarvey, were two of them.

Mr. Abrams had eyes that smiled. I knew he had a great sense of humor as soon as I looked into them. He always laughed at the little notes I wrote to him about things I thought were funny. Not everyone appreciated a seventh grader's sense of humor, so I thought he was a real prince.

Mrs. Sarvey had me take spelling tests during my home-room period because she couldn't give me individual attention during class. She made it clear that although English was my best subject, I wasn't going to be coasting while she was my teacher. The more her students brought to class, the higher her expectations were for them.

Each week Mrs. Sarvey would write a new phrase in the corner of her blackboard. It was always an inspiring saying she wanted to pass on to us. I can still remember many of them—"when you get a lemon, make lemonade" or "triumph is just 'umph' added to 'try.'"

A lot of the class activities that were probably a nice change of pace for other students bored me silly. I watched my classmates listen to recordings of songs from the Civil War and watch films about the Revolution. I could only look at their faces and wonder what they were learning.

I couldn't understand or participate in most activities. When my class was assigned poems or stories to memorize and recite, I would commit mine to memory and then write them under the teacher's watchful eye. I was once so tired of the monotony of watching other students read their reports that I amused myself by starting an official foot change count. As the kids stood in front of the class, I wrote down how many times they changed their weight from one foot to another while they read.

My teachers operated under the illusion that a seat in front of their classrooms would enhance my speechreading skills. But those front seats allowed me to jump from understanding zero to understanding about twenty percent of their speech. I don't know whether they realized how much I was missing. Most of them didn't work with me one on one, and they judged my work only by how well I did on tests. If I didn't answer a test question correctly, my teachers could easily assume that I was to lazy to pay attention or do my reading, or that I was not smart enough to remember.

In class, I was rarely called on, and those few teachers who made the mistake of doing so did not repeat it. I wasn't sure whether they had called my name even if they were looking straight at me. After they made it clear that they wanted something from me, they still had to make me understand what it was. Then they had to try to understand my speech. It took more than the average amount of effort, so they took the path of least resistance and didn't bother.

There are people with hearing loss who have enough residual hearing to string together snatches of what they hear and couple it with speechreading to produce good results. I was not one of them. Most of my teachers made speechreading attempts hopeless, though some were interesting enough to make me want to watch them anyway.

In classes where I had teachers who were easy to speechread, I faced other obstacles. My teachers rarely sat or stood in one place for an entire class session. Some paced grooves in the classroom floor while giving me neck-craning workouts. And none of them had mastered the art of writing on the blackboard without turning their heads away from me to watch what they wrote. I never had a chance in math classes, where the solutions to most problems were explained while the teacher faced the blackboard.

On the rare occasions when I could follow a teacher in class, it was only for snatches here and there. I might pick up one sentence, but then I'd stumble over one that didn't make sense, and I was much too timid to ask the teacher to repeat it. This was high school. I was trying to fit in, not stand out.

In many of my classes, if I wasn't doing too well, a teacher would try to help by assigning another student to take notes for me. But finding a good notetaker was as tough as finding the perfect mate. People tend to take notes about the things they want to remember. What they want to remember depends largely on what they don't know. The odds of finding someone with a body of knowledge identical to mine never weighed heavily in my favor. One of the worst notetakers I ever had was assigned because she was the brightest girl in class. Her notes were poetic, but sparser than corn shoots in an Iowa drought.

Utopia for me would have meant finding a notetaker who could write everything; one with the stamina and attention span to scribble furiously for the entire class period. That never happened. The pen may be mightier than the sword, but the mouth moves a lot faster than either.

I did well in my classes because of the extra effort I put in and because my mother or Mr. Z sometimes intervened. He was still following my progress from a distance.

I routinely made the honor roll, and I was inducted into the National Honor Society, but my classes were by no means easy. In ninth-grade biology, for example, I was seated three rows back from the front. I was smack in the M's instead of up front where I usually sat with the kids whose last names came early in the phone book. Solely because of his position to my left, Steve Miller was assigned to take notes for me.

Those notes were incomprehensible. The teacher's lectures were more so, and the class did not follow a textbook. After the first couple of tests, I was scared out of my wits. I had taken tests that had questions I didn't understand, but never ones with questions about things I hadn't seen at all. I tried to adjust by kicking in the afterburners when I got home from school. I read everything I could find related to Steve's cryptic notes and the teacher's scribbles on the blackboard. For the first time in my life I was close to failing a subject.

Mom saw me struggle and knew I wasn't failing for lack of sweat. She loaded her mental six guns, hitched up the station wagon, and took off for a parent/teacher conference. I watched the event with the only other witness, Wyatt Burp, aka Fastest Tongue in the West, the frog who lived in the biology room's terrarium.

Mom's visit produced immediate results. In my next biology class, from what I could follow, the teacher publicly roasted Steve Miller for not taking better notes. I was humiliated to see the teacher dumping on Steve the responsibility for my success or failure in his class. And I knew my discomfort couldn't begin to approach what Steve was feeling. I was never able to look at him again without feeling guilty for the trouble I'd caused him.

But the teacher's outburst did get results. Others in the class were suddenly eager to lend me their notes, and the teacher made sure that I knew about all my assignments. I began to enjoy biology, and my test scores shot up.

At least two years of foreign language were mandatory for high school graduation. My parents arranged for me to study French with a private tutor who lived in Woolrich. I worked with her one night a week for about a year. By the time I was due to start French, in ninth grade, I had a pretty solid grasp of conjugation for the tricky French verbs.

My first high school French teacher, Mrs. O'Donnell, took pity on me. She looked at the scores on my first couple of tests and scrawled me a note saying there was no sense in repeating what I already knew. She gave me assignments from an advanced-level French textbook while she worked with the others in my class. I had tests alongside my classmates, but from a different book.

It was fun learning French on my own with official sanction. For once I had something interesting to do during a class. But the following year, I was assigned to take the French class under the department head. It was a radical change. The French teacher was a martinet; she had none of the warmth or flexibility I'd loved in Mrs. O'Donnell.

While she worked with the other students, I was assigned to read French literature in the school library, and then answer questions or write essays about it. I relished the challenge, and rarely made mistakes on my tess. But there was no pleasing this teacher. At the end of each grading period, she refused to give me an A because I couldn't use the language lab as the other students did. This was my first experience with a teacher who held me responsible for my deafness, as if I had some control over what I could hear. It upset me terribly.

My mother and Mr. Z discussed the grade with the woman, but she didn't budge an inch. The experience left such a bad taste that I refused to take French classes again until my final year of high school, after she had retired.

In order to graduate from high school, I developed a learning system that made my school day the opposite of everyone else's. During class time, I'd pay only enough attention to get an idea of what was being discussed and then I'd read pertinent parts of the textbook, if I could find any. If the teacher wrote "onomatopoeia" on the blackboard and I saw my classmates turn to page 45 of their books, I knew there was a connection.

When my teachers based their tests on what was in the textbook, I was safe. When they didn't, I had to work like a dervish to figure out what I was missing in my classes. Often that meant that work began in earnest after class.

I developed great skill at classroom hieroglyphics. I could read the notes of kids several feet away in any direction. Not only that, I could read them upside down and from many different angles. Sometimes the notes would give me clues about the class presentations. Other times they'd tell me about my classmates: "Shelley loves Jim" or "Beatles Forever."

Three things helped me to survive high school without going mad: daydreaming, reading, and writing. I never insulted my teachers by sleeping in class, but my daydreaming could take me hundreds of miles and many centuries from the room. I wrote stories and poetry, and occasionally I pestered my friends with notes.

Reading on the sly was my favorite occupation. I was a major league user of the school library. And I was on good terms with Miss Isabel Welch, the head of the community library, where I still took out seven books a week. During high school, I was in heaven because the school was only a short walk away from Miss Welch's. Often I could get permission to take my books back during study hall and pick up another seven.

It was not unusual for me to read two books a day. I tried to be discreet by hiding the book behind an open textbook or putting it in my lap. I probably didn't fool any of my teachers, but I wasn't taking any chances. Books were the one thing that relieved me from ever-threatening boredom.

7

Thank God for the slam book! I got a glimpse of one in junior high and knew I had to make my own. It gave me my first good view of the thoughts and interests of the kids I saw every day. The books were jerrybuilt by taking a pad of paper and putting a different question in each page: "What's your favorite song?" "What makes you want to puke?" They were my introduction to the fun of taking public opinion polls.

Since some of the questions were ones like "What's your least favorite class?" respondents had to be careful not to let the book get into enemy hands while they were writing. The name "slam book" could have come from how quickly the books were stashed when a teacher approached.

Some of my classmates became easier to speechread because they began to realize that they needed to talk to me face-to-face without mumbling. But high school was also the time lots of us had braces, and all that metal did weird things to the shape of the lips.

I "talked" with my friends largely by writing notes. No teacher ever caught me passing notes—or at least none made an issue of it. But it was a pretty unsatisfying form of communication because I couldn't get an immediate response to what I wrote.

I didn't have friends that I could hang out with. It wasn't that people didn't try to establish friendships. A lot did. I just wasn't good at building or sustaining a relationship because speechreading was so hard. I hated the stress of having to concentrate every minute. It was much easier to be by myself and free of pressure.

Like most high schools, mine had a lot of different "crowds." I liked my classmates no matter what group they belonged to. Maybe that explains why they selected me as their "D.A.R. Good Citizen" during my senior year.

I joined a lot of clubs because I liked variety and hands-on activities. I worked on the school newspaper and reported school activities for the local paper, the *Lock Haven Express*. I was on the yearbook staff and in the French Club, the Art Club, and the Future Teachers Club.

Volunteer work in the library was a great favorite; I stamped books, typed, and reshelved materials. For my assistance with publicity for class plays, I was rewarded with membership in the National Thespian Society.

When I had problems that seemed insurmountable, I went for long walks in the Woolrich woods. My journeys took me deep into the pine forests, but I never felt afraid. It was as if the trees sheltered and comforted me. When I couldn't get to the woods, I'd write. Finding a way to articulate my worries on paper helped me deal with them and see that they weren't as overwhelming as they'd looked. And as my writing skills improved, I entered and won several essay contests.

My Girl Scout badge collection started to gather dust. No adult stepped forward to serve as leader for the senior scout troop. For a while, I helped the director of my former troop. I liked the feeling that I had something to offer the younger children when they were working on crafts. Mom had encouraged me to do a Christmas project every year, making angels from old telephone books or decorations from doilies. I discovered that I liked designing things, and that led me to try other projects. The roses I made from tissue paper were such a hit that Mom asked me to teach her garden club the technique.

That popular teenage activity, babysitting, was one of the things I did plenty of during high school. Mom started to work part-time, saving money—college for four kids was no longer in the distant future. Gayle also started working, so I often cared for Randy and David. Randy was like Gayle had been, an easy kid to watch and entertain. David, unfortunately, took after me—he was a real hellion.

My sister was a hot commodity when it came to watching other people's children because she thought a babysitter was supposed to be a total homemaker substitute. She didn't just watch kids; she tidied up houses and did dishes. When she wasn't available, I was sometimes asked to take her place, and she always coached me to follow her example. I was good with kids as long as I could entertain them with books, television or my favorite games.

The parents whose kids I supervised placed a lot of trust in me. I had earned a reputation for keeping a cool head. I'd had lots of tumbles that drew blood, and whether the blood was mine or someone else's, I went about repairing the damage with little fanfare.

I won my parent's confidence one night when they took my brothers shopping, leaving Gayle and me alone. Gayle put her hand through a pane of glass while we were playing and severed an artery. She was bleeding profusely and the cut looked pretty ugly, so I went next door and asked an adult neighbor to drive Gayle to the doctor's office.

By the time Mom and Dad arrived home, Gayle was back, fully bandaged, and the glass and blood had been cleaned up. I was waiting in a cold sweat thinking we'd get hell for the broken window. I was dumbfounded and relieved when we got compliments on the way we'd handled things.

Since I had few opportunities for the usual teenage "girl talk" I thought I was the only teenager in my high school, if not the world, who had any problems. I once decided that if I had a boyfriend, I would fit in and be happy, so I spent many nights fruitlessly praying for one.

I won my President's Council on Physical Fitness badge every year in junior high and played every intramural sport offered in senior high—basketball, volleyball, and softball. I loved the feeling of being important to a team. Because I played with the same group of girls for three years, we knew each other's strengths and weaknesses well. We called our team the Purple Streaks, and by the time we were seniors, we had created a dynasty, placing first in every sport.

My high school had no interscholastic teams for girls, and we weren't at all happy about that. We tried to put together a track team and a tennis team, but we could never budge the bureaucracy.

Randy and David had become old enough to play sports, and we had great touch football games during the evenings in late summer and early fall. Dad would pair us four kids into teams and play quarterback for both sides just to keep things fair. Other kids in the neighborhood often joined us.

During high school, I was introduced to the delights of modern jazz dancing. My mother talked with Lindy Phillips, who was opening a dance school in Lock Haven, and signed me up for private lessons. Every Saturday afternoon, I'd work with Lindy before I went to the library.

Lindy's patience was equal to my clumsiness, and her enthusiasm for dancing was infectious. Her music choices were ideal for me; she used records that made it easy to memorize the pattern of vibrations. Her choreography was clever and fun to perform. When I was in tenth grade, I auditioned for the senior high variety show. I danced in a solo for that show every year, and I'm still remembered for a number called "The Fancy Feline," in which I mimicked the movements of a cat.

Weekends were the time I dreaded most during my high school years. I often went to the church recreation hall on Friday nights to play basketball or whatever game the other teens set up. I didn't always enjoy it, though, because boys ruled the place. If we played basketball, they rarely passed to a girl, and they liked to make the big plays. When we played volleyball, the boys would dart in front of the girls to get the ball first. It was hard to improve my skills when I never got to use them. And, unlike the other kids, I wasn't at the rec hall to socialize.

On Sunday nights I went to Methodist Youth Fellowship meetings. Gayle was also a member, and Dad served as the adult leader one year. They helped me enjoy a lot of activities.

I was happy to stay with my brothers on Saturday nights while Mom and Dad played cards with their friends. But my folks worried that I was such a retiring teenager; they didn't think it was good for me to spend my nights buried in yet another book while watching television with my brothers.

Several times my parents insisted I go to the YMCA dances in Lock Haven. Gayle would take me, with or without her current boyfriend, and then dance the night away.

The noise from all the people shouting at each other made it impossible for me to follow the music, and in the dark gym I couldn't even begin to try speechreading. I dreaded having to go to the dances. I was the most miserable of wallflowers.

My parents tried to help me make friends. One summer they encouraged me to have a slumber party. Mom and Gayle called several of the girls I liked and invited them to come for the night. It was a ghastly experience. We gathered our sleeping bags in my living room, the only place that really had open space, and I set about playing the hostess. The talk was moving fast, and I was barely holding my own with the group when my sister stopped by to see how things were going. My friends were fascinated by the attention of an older, more worldly girl, and were immediately drawn to her, as everyone always seemed to be. The more Gayle talked, the more I withdrew. She tried to compensate for me by becoming more charming. It ended up being Gayle's slumber party with my friends.

Gayle and I walked to school together, rode the bus together, went to Youth Fellowship together, and shared the same bedroom. She was the only person in my life who always seemed to be able to understand my speech and who was easy to speechread. If it was a royal pain to take me everywhere, she never complained. Unless she had a date or plans to meet a friend, I was usually welcome to tag along.

When Gayle left for college, I was devastated. I was a junior in high school at the time, and everything suddenly seemed frightening. I had always had faith that Gayle would watch out for me. She could hear the bus coming up the street and tell me to hurry. I knew that if I became sick at school, I just needed to ask for her and she'd make sure I got home. Nothing was the same without her. I went to Youth Fellowship and there was no one to explain the rules of a new game or tell me what to bring next week. Gayle had been my closest friend and the only person I routinely shared with. And I wasn't at an age where I wanted to do "girl talk" with my mother. I read my way through my last two years of high school because there wasn't much else I enjoyed doing without Gayle.

Kathy Arndt got me interested in big books during my last year of high school. I had seen her in some of my classes, and I wanted to know her better because I noticed that she, too, was always reading. I rarely checked out library books of more than 250 pages because it was too hard to hide them behind a textbook and too tiring to lug them around. But Kathy was into Allen Drury's *Advise and Consent*, a hefty book with small print. I started to check out some of the books she was reading so that I would have some topics for conversations with her. I learned to love the depth in which characters and plots could be built in the bigger books, and gained a new friend in the process.

Unfortunately, Kathy lived in Lock Haven, and the only time we could easily see each other was at school.

In my senior year of high school, I went through a transformation. I finally got my braces off, and then I got contact lenses. I wore my hearing aid hidden in my bra and no longer felt like a machine with all its parts on display. Dad laughed when I told him that the makeover was my contribution to Lady Bird Johnson's "Keep America Beautiful" campaign.

8

To give me a taste of what I'd be up against after high school, my parents persuaded Lock Haven State College to let me take an English class. Although I didn't know it, I was also helping to prove something. A college administrator had told my parents that there was no way I could make it through college. I enrolled for the class during the summer before my senior year in high school. By that time, I had my driver's license and occasional use of the family car.

I found college to be much like high school. Class was just as boring. The big difference was that the students were all people I'd never met before. Nobody seemed to take notes, so I watched the classroom interaction and copied the few things that were written on the blackboard. As usual, my major work was done after class. It was tolerable because the subject material was interesting and challenging. The class gave me my first deep exposure to the strange mind of Lewis Carroll and the poetry of T. S. Eliot.

Because reading and writing had become my two favorite pastimes, I wanted to study either journalism or library science. There weren't many colleges in Pennsylvania that offered degrees in either field, but Pennsylvania State University had both. I also applied to Lehigh University, but predictably was turned down because it was an all-male school.

I knew my parents were concerned about my college choice. Penn State boasted a huge enrollment and large classes, meaning that my professors would be able to provide little or no attention to individual students.

Mom and Dad hinted that I might be happier elsewhere and took me to visit a couple of smaller colleges. But ultimately they left the choice to me. They had long since learned that when my mind was set on something, the intelligent thing to do was to get out of my way.

Mr. Z had gone to Penn State. He took me and my parents to meet with some professors. I never knew what they discussed, but by the time we left the campus, everyone seemed reassured that I would be all right there.

An added attraction of going to Penn State was its football team. I had followed the exploits of Lydell Mitchell, Franco Harris, Mike Reid, and Steve Smear with great interest. Dad had gone to some of the Nittany Lions home games with friends, since the campus was only about an hour away. I was looking forward to being a student at Penn State because I would be eligible for a season ticket dirt cheap.

I hadn't been away from my family since I became deaf, except for a few rare hospital stays and overnight visits with friends. Mom and Dad must have expected the college separation to be rough on me. The first day I was on campus, after they left, I walked over to find out where my mailbox would be. There were three letters in it—one from Mom, one from Gayle, and one from Dad. They'd been postmarked a day earlier in Woolrich.

I was touched, but I was also too busy to be homesick. I had been dying to leave for college. For as long as I could remember, I had been an oddity—the only deaf child in Woolrich, in my high school, and anywhere I went. I wanted to wear a different label.

The first day I hit Penn State, in June 1969, I knew that life was good. Walking to registration, I saw a woman with Ritz crackers hung on wires for earrings and an incredible, bushy red Afro. Seconds later, I noticed a man with clogs on his feet, beads in his hair, and clothes my family would disown me for. I was grinning by the time I had my classes lined up. On a campus with people this strange, I was going to seem mild by comparison.

My roommate was a former high school beauty queen and a first-class ego killer. She was very conscious of how she looked, and so was everyone else, especially men. At first, I followed her around like a puppy, making her friends mine. But we didn't have much in common, so I found other friends.

The study patterns I'd established in high school served me well in college. The only major difference was that college required a lot more work outside class. I made it much harder on myself by steadfastly trying to pass for a hearing person whenever possible. I rarely told any of my instructors that I was deaf. A few knew because there was no way to hide it.

I had decided to major in journalism, and I was surprised to find that there were no required classes in my major for the first year. Penn State's journalism department recognized that journalists would have to be versed in a wide range of topics, and expected that specialties were going to be very marketable. For this reason, journalism students were encouraged to carry a double major. After looking through the Penn State course catalogs, majoring in just one other field was the last thing I wanted to do. There were far too many fascinating things to study. I spent my years at Penn State trying to get a taste of everything I could.

My first semester brought some rough sledding. Most of my professors weren't working from a textbook. Few used a blackboard. And the seating and lighting made it nearly impossible to copy notes in the surreptitious way I'd learned during high school.

I had qualified for an advanced English class, which drew from a terrific mix of eclectic reading—*The Invisible Man, Candide,* and the *Book of Job* were a few of the selections. I was taken with the power of Ralph Ellison's words in *The Invisible Man,* especially his belief that "humanity is won by continuing to live in the face of certain defeat." Everything I read for the course gave me new worlds to explore. It was almost more than I could bear to go to class and sit in mute incomprehension while the others discussed the books.

My class in art history consisted of a series of slides on art and architecture that were shown in a huge room. The professor discussed the slides from a podium in the front of the room. The only light was from the slide projector. At first, I tried to memorize the slides by sight and then find them in my textbook or the college library. I'd read whatever I could find about the art, artist, and cultural period. I wasn't sure what I was supposed to be learning, but I tried to err on the side of excess.

After the first test, I knew that there were still too many things the professor was saying that I missed in my outside reading. I cultivated a friendship with another art history student who lived on my floor. She agreed to share her notes from the class. She also overheard the professor telling a student who had missed classes due to illness that a slide list would be posted outside his office following each class. Once I knew this, I didn't have to rely on my visual memory of each slide. Between the list, my friend's notes and lots of hours in the library, I pulled a B in the class.

At the other extreme, I had a biology teacher who was wonderful, too wonderful. I worried about his class from the first day because he was impossible to speechread, and I had bad memories of what had happened in high school biology.

I went to see the biology teacher right away and told him I was having trouble keeping up with his lectures. He sent me from his office with The Complete Biology Combat Kit. He gave me copies of his lecture notes and recommended a series of readings.

It took me hours each night to do the readings. In fact, I was spending so much time trying to keep on top of his class that I had to hustle to find time for the others. A lot of the articles he urged me to read were extraneous information that would not appear on the exams, but I never knew which ones might show up, so I read them all. When the semester ended, I was exhausted. But I had established myself. I knew that the high grades I'd enjoyed in the past were going to be tough to come by. Still, I was sure I could get through college.

My past tutoring in French and the attention from the good teachers I'd had paid off handsomely. I took a written test and scored high enough to be exempt from the required language courses. I didn't have to face the pressure of being unable to use the university's language lab.

My attempt to pass as a hearing student who was just like everyone else went to absurd lengths. I sacrificed a lot of things to keep up the pretense, including my grades. My Class From Hell was International Mass Communications, which met for hours at a stretch. It was all I could do to look interested during classes that were much shorter. I only attended classes to try to copy notes or be sure I wasn't graded lower due to lack of attendance. I had long since given up on trying to speechread my professors.

The Mass Communications course was taught by a very knowledgeable woman who seemed to be working her way through an encyclopedia, volume by excruciating volume. With so much information to absorb, *and no textbook to accompany it*, I was petrified. After a miserable score on my first test, I went to see the professor. Given the choice between failing a class and asking for help, I figured I could stand to beg a little. But she didn't give me her notes. I was horrified when she responded instead by going before the class and asking for someone to take notes for me. I felt as embarrassed as if she'd told them I had some sexually transmitted disease.

The more I acted like I thought a hearing person was supposed to, the more easily I seemed to be accepted and the more successful I felt. I was happy, even though my thinking was warped. The people around me might have liked me just as much without the pretense. But I was afraid to find out.

Just how far I was willing to go is illustrated by my behavior in a course called The Arts. The classes were held in an auditorium. Subject matter covered theater, film, and music. I watched live performances of *Waiting for Godot* and went to screenings of *Battleship Potemkin*.

The theater and film presentations quickly made me a lifelong fan. At the library, I could find scripts of the plays and reviews of the movies that helped me put in perspective what I'd just seen. From my professors, or, rather, from the people whose notes I copied, I learned about stage devices, montage, and *film noir*. But when the subject was music, everything became a mystery. I watched politely in class while pieces were played and discussed, only occasionally catching faint sounds or vibrations.

I studied everything about theater and film, no matter how trivial it looked. With music, I read what I could, though it had little meaning.

Every test gave equal weight to the three subjects. Some of the test questions about music referred to a piano passage that was played during the examination. The tests were multiple choice. For the music section, I'd pretend to listen with the other students, then I'd search the test sheet for an answer that looked most logical. I didn't always understand the question, so that wasn't much help.

I always aced the theater and film sections. I guessed enough right answers in the music sections to earn a C for my final grade. I was ridiculously proud of it. Not only had I passed that class without hearing and without help, but I'd been at least as good as an average student.

9

Thanks to Mr. Z, my parents knew that Penn State had speech and hearing services. They urged me to visit the clinic and see if I could get some help from the professionals there. I was loath to sign up for more punishment, but Mom and Dad were paying most of my college bills, and I wasn't about to bite the hand that fed me. I had a quick interview at the clinic. To my delight, I was told that my voice quality was superb for someone with the degree of hearing loss I'd experienced. The professionals there told me there was little they could do to improve my voice.

The speech and hearing department did, however, ask a favor. They were looking for people with hearing loss to participate in a study being done by some graduate students. I was eager to help, since it would mean that, for the first time, I could meet someone else who was deaf, unless I counted my hard-of-hearing grandmother.

I was introduced to the other volunteers in a group session. Ambitious, energetic Glenna planned to work with other people who had hearing loss. Tom was a sensitive, introspective man studying horticulture and working in the campus greenhouses. Entomologist John was a graduate student.

Denny, who rounded out the group, wasn't sure where he was headed but seemed likely to party his way there.

We hit it off immediately. Our group sessions continued long after the graduate students had the information they needed. For several months, we spent a lot of time together.

I was delighted to find people with whom I could drop my guard. All of us spent our days struggling to understand what was going on around us. We made sure we didn't struggle when we were with each other. We were strict about chewing gum and lighting and clear lip movements in ways we'd never dare to be with other people.

This little group gave me a chance to feel more positive about myself. Unfortunately, I squandered it. I kept comparing myself to the others and ended up feeling worse. Wherever we went, I watched Tom or Glenna or Denny or John interact with hearing people. When they ordered pizza or stopped to ask directions, they seemed sure of themselves. I was not.

I felt ashamed of my awkwardness. I had never really had an identity as a person who was deaf. I didn't understand that there are many degrees of hearing loss, and mine was far more profound than theirs. All of us wore hearing aids, spoke for ourselves, and used speechreading. However, I was the only member of the group who didn't have enough hearing to make telephone calls. I envied the others for their skill in doing that. I thought that I was just too stupid to train my ears as they had.

In April 1970, Glenna persuaded the rest of us to go to Washington, D.C., for a weekend. She knew someone who was attending Gallaudet College. I'd never heard of Gallaudet before, but I learned from Glenna that it was the only college in the United States designed specifically for deaf persons. To prepare us for the trip, Glenna taught us fingerspelling and a few signs.

We planned our arrival to coincide with the beginning of the campus Spring Carnival, an annual project by Alpha Sigma Pi fraternity. I was amazed that something with the name "carnival" could be so quiet, although the air was never still. Hands were swooping and slicing signs everywhere we looked.

It was my first exposure to people who had a hearing loss similar to mine. I felt like I was in an alien nation. I played Bingo and did a few other activities, but I was quickly worn out by the assault on my eyes from so much visual activity. Gallaudet, although it was designed for deaf persons, was an experience just like the hearing schools I was used to. Without a knowledge of signs, I was as lost around deaf people as I was around hearing ones.

At Penn State, I had my first real dates. I'd gone out with a couple of boys during high school, but it was more for friendship than a real date. I even had a "date" I arranged myself. I decided that once before I graduated, I wanted to know what a prom was all about.

I'd worked on the decorations for the senior prom, but I never summoned up the courage to ask any of the boys in my own class to take me. Instead I ended up asking a junior who was in my French class. The poor kid must have been petrified because he was out of school "sick" for a day before he came back and told me he'd go. He showed up with a corsage, but it was obvious he'd rather be anywhere else than at my prom. We spent a thoroughly uncomfortable evening seated at a table, watching everyone else have fun.

At Penn State, I conned a couple of guys who asked me for dates and never told them I was deaf. I thought it was hysterically funny when they equated my silence with shyness. But sometimes I gave wildly inappropriate answers to questions, or got labeled a snob because I didn't realize that my date was speaking to me.

Since a lot of women shared one telephone in the dorm, it wasn't at all unusual for them to take messages for each other. My roommates and friends took my phone calls and made arrangements for me to be picked up for my dates. None of the men I went out with had ever dated a deaf woman before. They weren't aware that my balance as well as my hearing had been affected by spinal meningitis. Beer was easy to get at parties, so they often assumed I was tipsy when I lurched around dimly lit areas where I couldn't get my bearings. Actually I didn't turn twenty-one until my last semester at Penn State, and I never drank because I was afraid to find out how much worse my balance might get.

On a campus of more than 30,000 people, deafness was still a novelty. People knew there was something strange about me, but they weren't sure what. Some thought my nasal speech was caused by a bad cold. Others guessed that I was from another country. All the guesses seemed much more acceptable than the truth, so I did little to enlighten them.

Debbie Brown and I were popular roommates on our floor during freshman year. We lived across from what was meant to be a study hall. Unfortunately, Penn State's administration had managed to underestimate the number of incoming students and the study hall had to be outfitted with cots for seven women. The hapless students in the study hall had no privacy, no closets, and sometimes no sense of humor. They stopped by our room quite a bit to gripe or simply to get away from their regular zoo.

One night the women from the study hall decided to have some fun. They staged a fake fire drill and I was the victim. Debbie was in on the whole thing; she woke me and said the fire alarm was sounding. I grabbed my bathrobe, dashed out the door, fell on my rear, and then slid for several feet. The study hall gang had greased the floor to make it slippery. When I realized I'd been had, I laughed hard and long, but the next day I got even. I covered the entire study hall with scented toilet paper. Then I stole Debbie's makeup and deodorant and forced her to go on a treasure hunt to recover them.

One of the study hall group, Charlita, was a serious Trekkie who watched "Star Trek" reruns every night in the dorm's television room. I often joined her, fascinated by her attraction to the series. Without knowing what the characters were saying, I thought the show was a bit on the pompous side. Then I saw the episode called "The Trouble with Tribbles" and knew I'd found a program that didn't take itself seriously. I was hooked.

My mother had been making broad hints that I should consider joining a sorority. I thought all Greeks were stuck-up clones, but I was willing to humor her by at least experiencing the rush process. It helped that Debbie and most of the study hall gang also signed up for rush and we'd be going together. Penn State had about thirty sororities, and rush was an ordeal because rushees were required to complete it in one week. The first two nights, we had to visit every sorority for a few minutes. By the end of the week, we could narrow down our visits to just a couple of sororities each night, and we spent more time with them.

My rush strategy was to be bright and cheerful, and, whenever possible, initiate the conversation. This gave me a fighting chance to know what the topic was, which in turn improved my ability to speechread.

I was surprised to find that I enjoyed the atmosphere in two or three of the sororities. The women seemed to be as close as families, but much more polite. I decided I was ready to become a Greek. At the week's end I had received three bids. It was a tough choice, but Karen Barth gave Kappa Delta the edge. She had been my sister's closest friend in high school, and whenever I visited Kappa Delta she made me feel welcome. Later, Karen became my roommate and did a great deal to expand my thinking with her open-minded view of life.

The sisters of Kappa Delta filled an important void for me. When I became part of their family, I sensed a feeling of being accepted that I had deeply needed. It was exciting to be part of a group with people from so many backgrounds, who had a variety of interests, and an explosive mix of personalities. I learned that even those women I would not have chosen for my friends had wonderful qualities that should be cherished. It was one of the most valuable lessons I learned in college.

Besides football, Penn State had a heady mixture of other sports with low admission charges. I went to soccer, basketball, gymnastics, and other events. One of my boyfriends was a rugby player who introduced me to his crazy sport and the more important post-game parties. A number of my sorority sisters were excellent athletes, and I followed their progress with interest.

My first year at Penn State, I auditioned successfully for a group of campus dancers called Orchesis. There were about twenty of us in the group with varied dance backgrounds. I copied the movements in our practices and classes but wasn't always sure what I was supposed to be learning from them. I had never performed or studied alongside other dancers.

Orchesis was a major stretch from the school variety shows. Unlike the pieces Lindy Phillips had choreographed for me, these often had music without strong vibrations. This made them impossible to memorize. These dances weren't tailored to emphasize my strengths. I couldn't hold an off-balance pose for long unless I had some support.

There wasn't much I could do to improve my balance, but I discovered that dancing in an ensemble offered other ways to make up for my inability to memorize the vibrations. I simply memorized my position on the stage in relation to other dancers. If one of them was four paces from me and in a crouch, I knew I was supposed to start moving in the opposite direction with my arms in the air. If the other dancer's timing was off, mine was too.

From time to time, guest artists would visit Penn State, and I had the opportunity to attend master dance classes. Once, a prominent dancer and choreographer demonstrated exercises to build strength and flexibility. He had us lie on our stomachs and raise both hands and feet simultaneously.

While he walked around the gymnasium correcting flaws, I watched to see what his instructions would be. Unaware that I needed to raise my head to see his lips, the instructor strode to me, his face reflecting disapproval as he spoke about the need to keep my head down when I did the exercise. I didn't try to explain that I was speechreading but quickly lowered my head in compliance, so he knew that I understood. Unfortunately, when I looked up for the next instruction, he was still standing next to me and glaring. He took my action to be one of defiance. In the best King of Siam fashion, he placed a foot on my neck and firmly but not at all gently pushed my head to the floor. I was glad that my face was hidden, because it immediately flooded a deep crimson. I wondered if anyone would have the guts to explain to him that I was deaf. I sure didn't.

Popular songs had always fascinated me. In high school, I'd watched other kids swoon over the Beatles or Rolling Stones and wondered at the attraction. I often read magazine columns by music critics to try to find out what I was missing.

My sister, who was an outstanding singer and pianist, had introduced me to her changing favorites by playing them on the family piano. She went through phases, alternating oldies, tunes by Rodgers and Hammerstein or Burt Bacharach, and the latest popular hits. I loved to rest against the piano and feel the vibrations while I watched Gayle's body move in time to the music as she played and sang. When she left for college, I missed that contact with music. She had made it come alive for me.

The cultural life at Penn State was rich, and student tickets at first-class events were very affordable. When I heard that Arthur Rubinstein would be coming to the campus for the cultural series, I was anxious to see him perform.

I had a game plan. I wanted to reach the auditorium early and stake out a seat as close to his piano as possible. Arriving at the concert hall, I sensed disaster. The seats closest to the piano had been roped off for dignitaries and major patrons. The closest ones available were on the balcony overlooking the stage. I settled in one, fingers crossed.

An hour later, as Rubinstein caressed his way through the first piece, I had more bad news. No sound carried from the stage to my hearing aid, and the composition of the balcony permitted no vibrations. Moreover, seated high and to one side, I could not get a glimpse of Rubinstein's hands.

I became more depressed by the second. I had come with such high expectations! It seemed that I was condemned to brood while others enjoyed what I couldn't. I was miserable, and I struggled to hold back tears. I didn't want to upset the music lovers around me and spoil the experience for them. And I didn't want to be rude and walk out during such an electrifying performance.

As I waited for intermission, overwhelmed by self-pity, a curious thing happened. A subtle movement drew my eyes to the knee of the person seated next to me, where fingers stroked imaginary keys as their owner dreamed of creating such music. I looked in the opposite direction. Another movement, feet tapped quietly but with gusto.

I glanced at those who sat in front of the piano, where I'd hoped to be. And I smiled. Heads nodded in time to the music, dipped for the low and high notes, and shook at sudden, intense passages. Faces were upturned, eyes half-closed; some were so transparent that they registered the raw emotion of the piece.

Maybe I couldn't hear the music, but I could see it. It was the performance of Rubinstein's lifetime, translated in perfection by the bodies of those around me. At the end of the evening, my vigorous applause was for the audience as well as the pianist.

Years later, ironically, I watched John Rubinstein, Arthur's son, gain great fame as a stage actor. The acclaim came for his work in a play about deafness—*Children of a Lesser God*.

—————————10—————————

Sororities at Penn State occupied floors in the campus dorms, but fraternities had houses off campus. I had gone out several times with a brother from Pi Kappa Phi after being introduced by one of my sorority sisters. The relationship didn't work out, but my friendships with the other Pi Kapp brothers continued. During my sophomore year, I was made a Big Sister and paired with a new Pi Kapp pledge, Jerry Druck.

Jerry was a ton of fun. He was the brother I'd always wanted. I could speechread him easily. Randy and David were getting to the age where they could sometimes be understood, but their interests were far different from mine. Jerry's interests could best be described as eclectic, and he liked to involve me in them. He was very persuasive; he could get me to help him practice folk dancing in the hall of my dorm, give haircuts to him and the other pledges, or spend all night shooting the breeze in a coffee shop.

I often went to Pi Kapp house on weekends when I didn't have a date. During my visits, I found myself drawn to a tall, quiet brother who seemed to be watching everything from a distance. I felt his eyes on me many times.

Fred Heppner and I watched each other for over a year while we dated other people. He swears that when he first saw me, the thought crossed his mind "that's the woman I'm going to marry." I didn't have such a premonition, but I definitely felt a force pulling me in his direction.

We were hopelessly tangled whenever we tried to reach out. Fred had terrible difficulty understanding my speech, and it didn't help that I never knew how to project it over the din from the Pi Kapp television or the brothers talking in the background. I didn't have much better luck understanding his speech, either—his lips were virtually immobile because of his moustache.

But we kept trying to connect. Fred eventually was able to understand my speech. It took longer for me to catch on to his, so we exchanged elaborate pantomimes in the interim.

We started dating almost as a cosmic fluke. I had been dumped for the first time by a guy I was hopelessly attached to, and I wasn't at all anxious to start another relationship. I figured Fred was a safe person to go out with. I was very attracted to him, but there seemed to be a lot of reasons why the relationship wouldn't last. He was in ROTC and on his way to becoming an officer in the Navy; I was antimilitary and antiwar.

I thought Fred was one of the most stable people I'd ever met. Everything about him fairly shouted responsibility and quiet strength. He was always on time for dates; in fact, he had a maddening habit of arriving ten to fifteen minutes early and making me feel like I had to rush because *I* was late. I liked his level-headed approach to things, but I was afraid he might be deathly dull to be around in the long run. As it turned out, Fred was a Renaissance man. His intelligence was incredibly wide-ranging, and he could talk to anyone about anything.

I especially liked Fred's attitude about my deafness. He wasn't pitying and he didn't make me feel like a freak. He had a matter-of-fact way of thinking, a sort of "so it's there, what else is new?" approach. He also had a wonderful, disarming sense of humor when things went wrong because I couldn't hear.

Our early dates were of the Jekyll/Hyde variety. I'd go out, have a wonderful time, and then get scared as I realized I was getting more attached to Fred. We had a lot of fights as we tried to find a good reason to terminate our relationship. Nothing significant came to mind, so we got engaged.

Fred was a year older, though, and before we could marry we had to endure a separation while I finished school and he started his Navy career. He was sent to Key West for training and then to Vietnam for a tour aboard the *U.S.S. Davis*, a destroyer. Our letters during this period were prolific, and we kept growing closer.

When Fred returned from Vietnam, was one semester short of graduation, but I only needed six credits. I arranged to complete my requirements through independent study. We had a small wedding in Woolrich Community Church on January 27, 1973, and then moved into the apartment Fred had found for us in Newport, Rhode Island, where his ship was stationed.

Fred and I never knew the dire statistics about "mixed" marriages between deaf and hearing persons or the fact that 90 percent of deaf persons marry others who are deaf. We were the fools who rushed in. Even if we had known about the unhappy fate of other couples who ignored the statistics, it probably wouldn't have made an impact. I felt immune because I thought of myself as a hearing person.

Nobody had told us that life together would be easy. But we never anticipated that it would be so hard.

I didn't adjust well to Navy life, which was highly traditional and blatantly sexist. Wives were expected to sacrifice almost everything to support their husbands. They had to be strong and independent to survive the separations. But when the husbands arrived home, the wives were expected to hand over all the things they'd learned to do—and sometimes do well. The husband ruled the roost when he was in town.

Simple things like being together with Fred became complicated for me. At first, on the evenings when he had shipboard duty, Fred would invite me to dinner in the officer's wardroom so that we could see each other. The wardroom rules made me crazy, and Fred, unfortunately, never briefed me on them. I learned them through on-the-job training.

It was the role of the highest ranking officer to entertain guests, including wives. I was always seated to the right of the big cheese at the head of the table. I was the first to be served by the steward. No one could eat until I had started to do so, a rule that I learned when I looked out on a table full of hungry faces staring first at me and then their plates. I looked to Fred and saw him mouth the word "eat" while making a slight nudge with his head, the kind a mother dog gives to encourage a reluctant pup.

Second helpings couldn't be brought, nor could anyone leave the table, until I had finished my meal. But I found it impossible to eat *and* be a good guest. I couldn't carry on a conversation while forking and cutting food. I had to look at a speaker so that I could speechread. And when it was my turn to respond, I didn't want to be chewing and speaking at the same time.

Many of the officers wolfed down their food quickly so that they could get back to work or leave for another activity. My food, by comparison, was barely touched by the time they finished. I usually ended up saying that I was finished and sending my food back to the kitchen with the steward. It was better than having the officers staring at me while they fidgeted.

To add to the stress, I couldn't speechread a number of the senior officers who hosted the meals, and I was deathly afraid of embarrassing Fred. The meals were so structured that I really didn't have time to talk to my husband, which was the whole point of coming to the ship. After a couple of meals in the wardroom, I decided it wasn't worth the effort.

I left those wardroom meals hungry, but Fred fared much better at keeping his stomach filled. I rose each morning at 6:00 or 6:30 a.m. to cook breakfast for him before he left for the ship. It was two months before he confessed that he was double dipping—breakfast was also being served on the ship when he arrived!

Our move to Newport brought a total change in our roles. I had always been a shy person, and I thought Fred was too. In college, I'd played at being an extrovert, patterning my behavior after my sister Gayle. It was easy to act outgoing around people I knew and was fairly comfortable with. I started Conga lines at parties and struck up conversations with strangers. In Newport, surrounded by strange people in a strange state, my shyness took over. Fred's extroverted side, of which I'd seen litle, suddenly displayed itself and, over time, he became more comfortable being the instigator.

We couldn't ignore the things that happened because only one of us could hear. Fred had to learn a new set of rules for polite behavior. When I was curled up in a chair, totally enthralled by a book, the worst thing he could do was to whack the chair to get my attention. Even a slight tap had the impact of a ship slamming full speed into an iceberg.

From Fred I learned more about the rules of the hearing world. I had to be careful that I didn't crack my gum or make loud gulping noises when drinking.

I was amazed to discover Fred's slavery to the telephone. He couldn't bear to let it ring. No matter how absorbed he was in something, he'd rush off as if lives depended on his quick response to a call. The telephone wasn't his only master, dripping faucets and squeaky doors that I wasn't aware of could drive him to distraction.

Our apartment in Newport was right outside the base, and it was nothing like the college dorm I was used to. I was living in a building with people I didn't know and rarely saw, and many of them were not connected to the Navy.

At first, because I hadn't made any friends, I depended heavily on Fred. He would come home beat from being packed tight on a ship with people who made constant demands on him. His deepest wish was to be left alone. By contrast, I'd spent my day without any companionship and I was dying to have someone to talk with. It took me a while to realize that I needed to give Fred an hour by himself when he first arrived, and that his less-than-enthusiastic listening during that time didn't mean that he didn't love me.

We had been married about three months when Fred left for a routine cruise that turned out to be anything but. His ship started sinking, so it headed for the nearest port. That turned out to be Charleston, S.C. I was sitting in our apartment reading a letter from Fred explaining that he was stuck in Charleston when I noticed a movement in the room. I looked up to see Fred walking toward me. It was no apparition. He'd found out that the ship would be in dry dock for at least two weeks and had arranged to take a plane home and drive back to Charleston with me. I quickly threw some things in a suitcase and we headed south to reach Charleston before his leave ran out.

The ship's damage was more extensive than anticipated. The two weeks eventually stretched to two months. It had been late winter when I left Rhode Island, and I'd packed only heavy clothes. Within two weeks, the South Carolina sun provided 90 degree temperatures by 9 a.m.

Fred and I were allowed to room together at the Bachelor Officers Quarters (BOQ) on the base. It was ridiculously cheap at $2.50 a day, but the rooms had only two twin-size beds since, after all, they were designed for bachelors. We tried putting two beds together, but one of us always seemed to be kissing the floor in the middle of the night. We ended up crammed into one bed for safety. Sharing a small bed with a 6'4" man for two months required real love. So did dealing with the steward.

Since the officers had to be aboard ship early each morning, stewards would come to clean their rooms at about 6:30

a.m. I had to vacate our room so that it could be cleaned, but there was nowhere to go, since stores and libraries didn't open for another three hours.

I'd left my college course work in Rhode Island because I thought I'd only be gone for two weeks. The base library was small but provided escape from boredom. Eating every meal out was not so easy. It became monotonous fast, and I discovered it was possible to deeply crave being able to cook.

Fred was the junior officer on his ship, and he was invariably stuck with shipboard duty for every holiday. On Memorial Day, the base was so deserted that we watched *Krakatoa, East of Java* in the theater with only three other people before Fred went on duty. But I loved being in Charleston.

Within a week after I arrived, other officers' wives from Newport started to register at the BOQ. Many of those who came were also childless and no happier about the Navy's sexism and inflexibility than I was. I could communicate easily with several of them, and it was blissful to make friends again. We played tennis in the morning, watched "All My Children" in the afternoon, and talked often. By the time we all returned to Newport, I had friendships that were solidly established.

That summer, several of our Charleston wives' group offered to work as assistant counselors at a Girl Scout camp. We drove across the magnificent Newport Bridge each morning and made enough money at the camp to pay the toll on the way back at night. Charlene Reilly, one of the wives, also found me some occasional work as a bookkeeper for the landscaping business owned by her landlords.

When our husbands were away, we would arrange to have dinner together every night. Anyone who wanted company was welcome to show up. We took turns hosting the dinners and cooking specialties from the regions we'd been raised in. Since we came from all over the country, it was a great chance to learn to cook each other's favorites. I tasted my first okra, spiced shrimp, and tacos at those dinners.

Gradually my wonderful group of friends dispersed. Some were leaving the Navy as they completed the years they'd committed to serve. Others were being reassigned to different ports. In the meantime, I was finding that the long separations were easier to tolerate than the short ones.

When the ship went out for extended cruises, the officers' wives pulled together and created a strong support system. But the short cruises of just a few days, designed to test various shipboard systems, were much more frequent and more stressful. When the men were at home, they were often obsessed by details of things that needed to be done before they left again.

I couldn't touch base with Fred by the usual ship-to-shore phone when he was away. Letters were pointless because we'd be back together before they would arrive. In many ways it was harder for Fred to be incommunicado than it was for me. He felt responsible for my safety and hated not being able to get in touch and make sure that I was all right. It bothered him so much that he decided to apply for shore duty on humanitarian grounds.

Advancement in the Navy depends heavily on experience aboard ship. Fred crushed any chances for a good career when he pushed for shore duty. I hated having to appear helpless so that his request would be granted, and I resented that he was being forced to make the choice between me and his career. But I was relieved when his request was granted and he was assigned to the Naval Officers Training Center on the base.

11

I had completed the course work for my independent study program soon after my return from Charleston to Newport, but graduating from Penn State took longer than I had planned. Fred arranged for me to have a proctored final exam on the base so I wouldn't have to drive back to Penn State. The officer in charge never sent in my test results. I didn't find out until the day of graduation, when my parents were contacted by my faculty advisor. The missing test results were eventually located, and I received my degree at the end of the following semester, in the fall of 1973.

I was eager to enter the world of work. I'd had a few jobs during college, always gained through my parents' contacts. I had done summer work at Woolrich Woolen Mills, where I risked blindness inspecting and packaging dayglo-colored hunting jackets along with the more traditional coats. The mill was generous about hiring college students, just as it was like an extended family in other ways. Woolrich, Inc. had been good to our family and others in the town with its sponsorship of the church, fellowship hall, park, little league field, and many other things I had enjoyed while growing up. During Christmas holidays, I'd picked up pocket money working with Mom in an elegant women's clothing store called The Smart Shop.

Penn State had helped me focus on what I really wanted to do. I liked writing, but I found out quickly that with my limited speechreading abilities, reporting would be out of the question. I planned instead to become the next Peg Bracken or Erma Bombeck. Both writers were favorites of mine for the humor they found in mundane things. But after I took a class in editing, I was sure I had found my calling.

I enjoyed doing things to improve the writing of my peers, and I loved using the skills and judgment required of a good editor. What I liked most about editing work, though, was that it was chaotic. Writing a piece involved researching and reporting one area. Editing called for keeping track of many areas being written about at the same time. Editors were bombarded with information. My mind was already honed for constant sifting of information and making judgment calls. I was eager to put my talent to use.

My parents believed in me. My teachers believed in me. My husband believed in me. And I believed in myself. Naively secure, knowing that I had skills of great value, I was totally unprepared for the job hunt. I quickly discovered that expertise was no match for the misperceptions held by many employers.

In Newport, I couldn't call on family or friends, those mother lodes of job leads. The closest relatives lived four hours away, and I'd only just started to make friends. I wasn't worried at first, because I felt sure my talents would speak for themselves.

But I came up against prejudice immediately. Newport's economy was fueled by the tourist industry and by support services for the Navy base. Professional jobs for women were hard to come by, especially for military wives. Employers saw the Navy wife as a bad employment risk. Families were constantly being transferred, and the wife had to shoulder a lot of extra responsibilities when her husband was at sea.

Add the extra baggage of my deafness and I got a triple whammy—I was a woman, a Navy wife, and disabled. After a few rebuffs when I sought professional jobs, I knew that I would have to set my sights lower. I could live with that, since I knew one job could lead to others.

I searched in earnest, but things did not improve. Some employers invited me for an interview. Communication was awkward, and sometimes the discomfort of my interviewer was obvious. I was also uncomfortable, frustrated by my inability to speechread accurately and put them at ease. I bluffed heavily if I wasn't sure of what they said.

I was also encountering blatant discrimination. I would be told that a job was filled, then pick up my newspaper and see it advertised every day for the next week.

Desperation made me grovel. After several weeks of fruitless searching, I offered to work for free for a week, two weeks, or a month if an employer would only give me the chance to prove myself. I didn't have any takers for my offer, and I was devastated.

Eventually I reached the point where one more rejection would have destroyed what was left of my self-esteem. I couldn't risk it. I announced to Fred that I had decided to devote more time to some projects I was doing at home. He wasn't fooled, but he didn't push me to look for work again. I dedicated myself to an all-out attempt to be a good Navy wife.

Those four years were like a long journey across a desert. For a time, I did a fair job of convincing myself that I was happy. But I wasn't cut from the traditional mold, and I wanted to do more than be a good wife to someone.

After Fred started shore duty, we knew that we could count on being in Newport for the next few years. We moved from our small apartment to a townhouse in the military housing area. We didn't have much furniture, but the move was complicated because we did have twelve tanks full of tropical fish.

I missed the group of wives whose husbands were on Fred's ship, but the move gave me opportunities to make new friends. I quickly found others who shared our interests and were fun to be with. John and Vicki Kniering went with us to visit fish stores. Vicki was a talented artist who was always eager to take trips to exotic places. We also shared many good times with Ken and Linda Bishop. They were sports fans, and Linda persuaded me to join a bowling league.

Military housing had no restrictions on pets, and I was delighted when Fred gave me a Shetland Sheepdog puppy for Valentine's Day in 1974. I named her White Ruff Toby. My little Sheltie was clever and energetic, and she quickly took over my life.

There were no hearing dog programs back then, but I took advantage of Toby's working dog heritage, intelligence, and sensitive hearing to learn all kinds of information. She loved both the Scottie next door and young Siegfried, the Knierings' miniature schnauzer. But Toby was especially partial to our mail carrier, who always had dog biscuits in his pocket. It wasn't long before she'd rush to get me, barking excitedly, whenever someone came to the door. She wasn't about to miss a chance to get a biscuit, and I made sure to praise her or give her a treat if the caller wasn't the mail carrier.

We had only one car; sometimes I drove Fred to work so that I could use it during the day. Toby and I liked to go for walks on Newport Beach or the famous Cliff Walk. The only drawback to having the car was in arranging to pick Fred up after work. We worked out a special telephone signal. He would dial our home telephone number and let the phone ring twice, then hang up, dial again, and let it ring two more times. When I heard the signal, I would pick up the receiver and tell him I was on my way.

To be ready for his calls, I would sit near the phone with my hearing aid turned up as high as I could tolerate. Since I never knew what time he might call, I sometimes had to wait an hour or more.

I took Toby with me when I went to pick up Fred. I would tell her that we were "going to get Daddy." Soon she associated the phone calls with the joyful trip in the car. She got excited whenever I was home alone and the telephone rang. She'd bark, come to find me, and lead me to the telephone. Toby's actions freed me from the slavery of long waits for phone calls.

We also took Toby to obedience school, where she quickly learned the basic commands and became a star pupil. We were amused when she was tapped to be in a PBS show filmed in Newport. The British Broadcasting Company was filming a re-creation of the black tie dinner for dogs given by Mrs. Stuyvesant Fish in the 1890s at her house on Ocean Drive. Toby wore a pink bow and stood across the table from a monstrous Golden Retriever who cast covetous looks at her plate. As the film rolled, Toby wisely decided to take a few paces backward and let the Golden Retriever fill his belly from both of their plates.

I played midwife for Toby's first litter, and we kept one of the pups, White Ruff's Tam o' Shanter, whom we called Tammy for short.

Mom and Dad were still going to Maine every summer, and Fred and I often joined them. Fred had developed great fondness for lobsters, especially the ones at Dad's favorite hangout, Cook's on Bailey's Island.

Gramp McIntosh had passed away and was buried in the cemetery for which he'd once provided such exquisite care. We still split our Maine visits between their house in Lisbon Falls and the farm in Waterville, with side trips for the July 4th re-unions and one good day at Old Orchard Beach.

I'd finally figured out the secret behind Gram Mac's fa-mous diet. Every few months she'd write, and she always bragged that she was doing well losing fifteen pounds on her doctor's advice. She'd been telling me that for more than ten years, and whenever I saw her she never looked any thinner. Moreover, she could put away food with the best of us. Eventually it dawned on me that she was repeatedly gaining and losing the same fifteen pounds.

Fred became lead instructor at the Instructor Training School and met many interesting people. During fall and winter, he competed in the base basketball and volleyball tournaments. His teams were very successful. I went to all his games and some of the practice sessions. I was dying to play myself, but there were no organized sports for women on the base.

Fred often went to represent the base in interbase competitions. One night while he was out of town for a tournament, Toby woke me. She was sleeping on the bed, wedged against my legs. I could feel growls start low in her throat and build. I knew instinctively that someone was in the house.

As her body tensed, ready to spring, I understood that the intruder was heading toward us. My heart was hammering its way out of my chest. I saw a dark shape outlined in the doorway and was preparing to scream when Toby's body relaxed and I felt her tail wag against my legs. Fred had decided to surprise me by leaving early and driving through the night so that we could have the next day together. His "surprise" earned him one heck of a tongue-lashing.

While driving near Providence, Fred and I discovered a quaint boatyard with many unique sailboats. It reminded Fred of the fun he'd had as a child, when he'd sailed on the lake near his grandfather's cottage in Connecticut. He fell hard for a 24-foot all-wood sloop that was sadly in need of restoration. It wasn't long before he owned it.

I spent most of an entire summer scraping and painting the boat's fir, oak, and mahogany to restore it to its original splendor. I was appalled by the cost of materials and dismayed by how much work was required. As a reward for my "sweat equity" I was permitted to name the boat. I chose Loki after the the Norse god of discord and trouble.

The daily round trips to Providence to work on the boat were grueling. Eventually Fred sailed Loki to a mooring in Newport Harbor. But it wasn't as easy to work on a rocking boat as it was in the dry boatyard. I was almost trapped overnight once when I couldn't raise the harbor taxi to come and pick me up. I kept signaling with my foghorn, but I couldn't tell if anyone was answering me.

While we had the boat, we spent so much time working on it that we rarely had the luxury of taking it out to enjoy a sail. On the few times we actually sailed it, Toby was by far the most thrilled. She loved to run across the deck, and she was amazingly sure-footed even when the boat was slick with spray. She never tired of trying to protect us from seagulls as she trotted fore and aft.

When Toby wasn't spinning around the deck, her favorite place was behind Fred as he steered. Once Fred forgot about her while tacking. With a quick sweep of the tiller, his elbow shot out and knocked Toby clean off the boat. She disappeared in the dark blue ocean, sinking quickly from sight as her thick coat absorbed water and weighed her down. When she suddenly resurfaced, we hauled her aboard, worried that she'd be spooked by the experience. To our relief, she gave two vigorous shakes of her coat and went right back to patrolling the deck.

Several times Fred brought home work from students at the Naval War College, which was also located on the base. The students needed help writing and editing their papers. I earned some pocket money and learned a few things about naval warfare that I'd never wanted to know.

From time to time, I put out feelers for a job. In 1975, a written inquiry to the Newport Council for International Visitors brought a call from the director. She had fond memories of a person whose name was similar to mine and who had also graduated from Penn State. Although I wasn't the person she'd hoped to find, she was in need of a volunteer to handle the Council's public relations work. I ended up serving as publicity director, revamping a number of the materials.

It was exciting work. The Council was gearing up to host the bicentennial visit of the Tall Ships in Newport Harbor. I worked with them to find hundreds of volunteers to pull off the visit. It was great to be back in my field, pay or no pay.

My brother David and a friend of mine from high school, Cindy Shaffer, came to stay with me during the event. David was becoming a truly astonishing kid. Everything I did, he did too—only better. When I taught him to make pizza, he made ones that were works of art. Cindy had stayed in touch with my family and was interested in the Tall Ships events because she spoke Spanish quite well and some of the ships were from Spanish-speaking countries. She had been an exchange student in Argentina for a year.

I worked at the Volunteer Center and took David and Cindy to visit some of the ships in the harbor. We met a terrific sailor, Luis Manuel Evora Bonito, from the Portuguese ship and brought him home for a party when we found out it was his birthday. Fred was involved in the Tall Ships events as well, serving as liaison to the Polish ship, *Dar Pomorza*.

The exposure to people from other countries made us realize how fortunate we were. We had bought a second car, a sickly, beat-up, paint-faded Volkswagen Beetle, which Fred used to take one of the Polish sailors to a Tall Ships meeting. The sailor was impressed. He thought we were wealthy because we had two cars and a townhouse with two bathrooms.

During my free time in Newport, I read my way through the base library and then the Middletown library, which was about a mile from where we lived. I learned it is not a good idea to read *The Exorcist* when one's husband is away at night. I studied psychology, reincarnation, gardening, tropical fish breeding, dog training, and anything else that took my fancy.

In 1976, Fred's military obligation was completed. I looked forward to a new life and a chance to do real work. The memories of my first job hunt had lost their hurtful edges and I was ready to make a new start in a new place.

12

Fred was offered a position as a pharmaceutical representative for Pfizer Laboratories in a territory that covered the northern Shenandoah Valley of Virginia and parts of West Virginia and Maryland. Pfizer had experienced problems keeping that sales position filled, and the district manager encouraged us to visit the area before making a decision. We'd heard the valley was beautiful but had never seen it. We drove to Winchester, Virginia, the central point of the territory, to find out what it was like.

We fell in love with Winchester immediately. It was much bigger than Woolrich but smaller than the West Nyack area of New York in which Fred had been raised. We liked the tree-lined streets and the hospitality of the people we met. It didn't take long for Fred to accept the job and send for our things in Rhode Island.

We rented a ranch house, with an option to buy if things worked out. While Fred studied medical texts and terminology, I hunted for a job again. At the local Employment Commission office, I learned about an opening for part-time work at the Virginia Book Company. My job turned out to be largely indexing and typing, but it was a start. Stuart Brown, a studious and courtly country lawyer, owned the company, which published histories and genealogies. Later I began to type and edit manuscripts for his wife, who wrote children's books and stories.

The work didn't keep me busy, but the owner of our house put me in touch with the vocational rehabilitation office. I went for an interview and was assigned to a counselor who seemed eager to help me. He looked first for a good match for my writing and editing skills, but came up empty-handed. Eventually he was able to arrange for a temporary job at our local public library under the federal CETA program. The pay was less than minimum wage.

My first boss at Handley Library was Anne Lee, the technical services director. She told me up front that I was overqualified for the job, and she tried to find challenging things for me to do. I loved being around books all day, and several times Anne had to insist that I leave, or I'd have stayed at work all night as well.

As the person who processed new books, I was one of the first to see everything that came in. I developed a whole slew of new interests from the books that passed my desk, and it was a rare day that I didn't go home with one or two to read.

I saw the first evidence of failed mental health policies at the library, after deinstitutionalization planted the seeds of what would later become a large population of homeless persons. At the library, there were people who had no place to go. They would come early in the morning and stay until we locked up. I never knew where they went when we closed.

Colorful local characters were as much in abundance as books. A thin, quiet woman in her early twenties came to the library often, always with the same question, "What do you have about Elvis?" She eventually discovered science fiction, but not before I had fantasized that she'd fall hopelessly in love with our Elvis look-alike. He was another frequent visitor of about the same age. He didn't wear sequined jumpsuits, but he had his hair done in a passing imitation of the famous ducktail. Only his makeup and scent spoiled the effect. We knew instantly when our Elvis clone was in the library. The reek of his cologne traveled faster than the speed of light.

We had slashers, too, but of a different sort. For weeks before he was caught, a mild-mannered gent neatly cut the stock reports from our newspapers with a razor blade. And we saw a slight, middle-aged man in sloppily laced hightop sneakers sneak around stealing the scrap paper and golf course pencils we placed near the card catalog.

The town fathers and the library board had haggled for years over an addition to the crowded library building, reaching agreement about the same time I was hired. Until the addition was built, there was only one place I could work—in the children's room.

The library had no funds for a children's librarian, so I inherited the duties with the desk. Working there was especially tough for me because so many children were shy or couldn't tell me what they wanted. Some simply didn't know how to articulate their questions, others didn't yet know how to write well enough to give me a note. The kids were notorious for mumbling and other sins against speechreaders. They looked at their shoes or out the window while they talked. Some chewed gum; others chewed their fingernails.

I developed a librarian's sort of Twenty Questions. "Are you looking for a book?" "Do you like books with lots of pictures?" "Do you want a book about animals?" Since the kids were so tough to speechread, I instinctively asked questions that required only a head nod. With practice I was able to narrow things down quickly.

Like most persons with hearing loss, my visual powers had become strongly developed over time. I had phenomenal peripheral vision, and I could detect subtle movement. This made me a hard person to sneak up on. But in the cramped quarters of the children's room, it was possible for a short child's approach to be hidden by tables, chairs and shelves. The moppets scared the daylights out of me when they suddenly popped up.

Fortunately for the kids, I rapidly became skilled at recognizing their facial expressions and their body language—especially the kind that precedes "Where's the bathroom?"

Some parents viewed the library as a free babysitting service. I was fond of many of the children who were latchkey kids, and I enjoyed trying to steer them to books I hoped would get them hooked on reading. I started reading every new children's book before I placed it on the shelves. I wanted to be able to match books to the interests and reading levels of "my kids." I began to wax eloquent about some of my favorites, like the gentle "George and Martha" series and anything illustrated by Wallace Tripp.

The younger children didn't understand why I wasn't like the other adults they knew. Most hadn't yet learned prejudice. I explained to them that they needed to look at me when they talked and touch my arm to get my attention when they had a question. They accepted my directions without fuss.

I was saddened to see parents often stifling their kids' inquisitiveness. "What's that thing in your ear?" a child would ask, pointing to my hearing aid. Before I could answer, a horrified mother would yank the child away, flashing me a tight smile and apologizing profusely.

I knew what would come next; the child would get a stern lecture. The message that would stick was "Something is very wrong with this woman and you should not call attention to it." But I always welcomed the questions of children and tried hard to find ways to help them understand deafness. I knew that, for some of them, I would be their first exposure to a deaf person. I wanted to make it a positive one. They were my chance to help the next generation grow up without ignorance or misperceptions.

Fred and I had stayed active in dog obedience training. We joined the Blue Ridge Dog Training Club and sometimes worked Tam and Toby at practice sessions with the other members and their dogs. We assisted with the club's fun matches and tattoo clinics. Eventually Fred became President of the club and I started a club newsletter.

At Penn State, I'd had a class in photojournalism. I was fascinated with the way pictures could tell stories and how subtle changes in light or texture could affect the mood of a photograph. Fred had bought me a 35mm camera and several lenses. After we purchased our ranch house, he built a darkroom for me in the basement, where I worked happily while he rebuilt one of his many vehicles. Fred had developed a fondness for Alfa Romeo cars and Willys Jeeps, and we usually had several cluttering our driveway.

It was 1976. I was twenty-five years old with a good marriage, a job I liked, and a life I was becoming comfortable with. Toby and Tam had just had litters, and we'd kept two of the pups, which we'd named Mac and Leila. Fred's job was going well. We were making friends. My backyard garden provided a nice variety of summer vegetables. It seemed that I was headed for a quiet, comfortable life. Then I had two strokes and my world turned upside down.

The strokes were about two weeks apart. One of them destroyed the remaining hearing in my better ear. I went from having a profound hearing loss to having a more profound hearing loss.

I didn't immediately know what had happened to me. I'd been plagued for some time by headaches that were becoming more and more painful, but I chalked them up to the stress of adjusting to a new job. After the first stroke, which happened while I slept, I woke up feeling woozy. When I put my hearing aid on, it wouldn't work. I thought it was broken and that my dizziness resulted from the lack of familiar sounds. Fred and I drove two hours to reach the nearest hearing aid dealer who had experience with my brand of aid. The dealer couldn't find anything wrong with the hearing aid. But when he tested my hearing, I gave no response to sounds in my left ear—sounds so loud that he and Fred could both hear them from across the room.

My doctor had no explanation for the sudden loss, and I was still trying to adjust when the second stroke hit almost two weeks later. The headaches that preceded it were the worst I'd ever experienced, but I guessed that they were happening because the new hearing loss added to my stress level.

My library job helped me piece things together. I didn't realize that I'd had strokes until I scanned a new book as I prepared it for the shelves. The book was about problems associated with birth control pills, and I was curious about its contents. I was a birth control pill user, and both the doctors I saw and the magazines I read gave glowing reports of the pill's safety.

When I read the book's account of a woman who had experienced strokes, I felt a stab of recognition. Her recollection was a duplicate of my experience, and I was almost paralyzed with fear. I stopped using the pills immediately and had no more problems with headaches.

I was too overwhelmed by adjusting to care how fortunate I had been in losing just the hearing in one ear. I discovered that over the years I had learned to do hundreds of simple tasks by memorizing sound patterns. Although the quality of the sound was terrible, I had learned to associate it with my activities. When, after the strokes, I could no longer hear those sound patterns, I became totally disoriented.

There had been a rhythm for brushing my teeth. The toothbrush made a noise as I stroked it across my teeth, and it matched the vibration the bristles sent to my fingers. Without the familiar noise, I became clumsy. The toothbrush would fly toward my cheekbones and leave smears of toothpaste across my face.

My typing suffered too. At work, I had the reputation of being expert on my electric typewriter. I could quickly slip into a rapid typing pattern. Each time I pressed a key, my ears registered a sound and my fingers felt the impact of metal hitting paper. My new hearing loss changed all that. Suddenly I was no longer sure when a letter was printing; a push on any key gave neither sound nor vibration.

I had also taught myself to take cues from the dogs. Their barking took a distinct pattern when they sensed danger, and they knew I'd respond instantly to their warnings. There was a different cadence when they barked to let me know that Fred had arrived home. I was overwhelmed by the feeling of being isolated when I could no longer make the distinction.

By far the worst blow was to my hard-won communication skills. I had finally reached a point where I could speechread a few people with amazing accuracy. Many people had no difficulty understanding my speech as well. Using the constant reinforcement of what little hearing I had was critical to developing those skills. In one fell swoop, a stroke changed all that, wiping out eighteen years of work. My speech started to deteriorate again, and my speechreading skills plummeted.

I started having vivid nightmares, and suddenly the memories of things that happened after my first hearing loss came flooding back. I had done a good job of burying many painful and frustrating incidents, but I hadn't dug the hole deep enough.

In the morass, I was forced to confront myself. I didn't know if it would take me another eighteen years to regain my speech and speechreading skills. I didn't know if I had enough hearing left in my one working ear to even make it worth trying to find out.

I was filled with fear, but I wanted answers to those questions. The place where I could get the best answers was from other people who were deaf. I'd been so hell-bent on being like a hearing person that I didn't know any. I had seen a couple of deaf people in Winchester, but they communicated through sign language. I had no way to talk to them because I had long since forgotten the fingerspelling and the handful of signs Glenna had taught me for the trip to Gallaudet.

—————————————13—————

I turned to my old friends, books, for answers. I didn't always find my answers, but the books helped me to ask the right questions.

As I studied the library's meager collection of books about deafness, I began to realize that I was not a stupid person. Actually, I discovered, I was a darn good survivor. In high school I had compared myself to the kids around me. Even though my grades were high, I seemed to have to work much harder for them. I had never really understood that the other kids with good hearing had access to so much more information.

Glenna, Tom, Denny, and John had been able to use the phone and feel more comfortable with hearing people because they heard sound much better than I did. I hadn't known that hearing aid users could be so different in their ability to make sense of what they heard. I thought hearing aids were like eyeglasses and everyone's hearing got corrected to the same level. Instead, I found there was no such thing as "20/20 hearing." Hearing aids couldn't give us perfect hearing again.

I learned that there were different kinds of hearing loss. Nerve or sensorineural loss, which I had, was very different from conductive hearing loss. Turning up the volume on my hearing aid made the sound louder, not clearer. What I heard was little more than amplified gibberish.

Fred was as baffled by the intricacies of hearing loss as I was. He couldn't understand why, after my strokes, I couldn't just switch my hearing aid from my now-dead ear to the still-functioning one and pick up where I left off.

I was monumentally depressed, but I had always been a fighter and I wasn't willing to give up without one more battle. So I signed up for speech therapy at the local Easter Seals office. I was also becoming more curious about sign language. I wanted to learn it to see what the "deaf world" I was reading about was really like. I looked for a sign language teacher and eventually met a woman new to the area who knew signs. She was willing to teach a class. I helped get it set up at the community college so I could take it.

That first class in sign language was really comical. I was by far the worst student. The teacher and all the other students were hearing. I struggled to speechread them for over an hour, and picked up twenty or thirty signs that I could go home and teach to Fred in less than ten minutes. But it was fun anyway, and through the class I made a wonderful new friend, Tootie Campbell.

Quite by accident, I discovered that sign language was good for my speech. Bob Franz, my speech therapist, told me that I paced my speech much better and made sounds more distinctly when I talked while signing.

In 1979, shortly after I started learning sign language, I read in a newspaper announcement that Fred Yates would be in town to speak to the Lions Club. Fred was the director of the Virginia Council for the Deaf, a state agency. Until I saw the newspaper article, I didn't even know that such an agency existed.

I received permission from my supervisor to leave work to attend the speech. I also asked my sign language teacher, Cheryl Reames, to go with me. After his presentation to the

Lions, I introduced myself to Yates. In a real-life comedy of errors, because Cheryl Reames could sign and I could not, he thought that she was deaf and I was hearing.

I was delighted when Yates accepted my invitation to return with me to the library. He and I scrawled notes to each other at a table in the children's room until my arm ached. I was starved for information about deafness, and he was the first deaf professional I'd met. He recognized my need for answers and generously provided them. With Yates' encouragement and guidance, I began to understand how deafness had shaped my life.

About two months later, Yates asked me to attend a regional conference on mental health and deafness. There, I discussed weighty issues and pressing needs with a few deaf persons and a lot of hearing professionals. I learned about the damage done by people who wanted to play God, and we decried the lack of deaf professionals in the mental health field.

We needed people who understood what it was like to be afraid that we couldn't be good enough fathers or mothers to our hearing kids. We wanted to talk with people who knew about the extra pressure that came from having a boss who often gave instructions that could not be understood.

It was a heady, troubling, and enlightening experience to attend that conference. I felt a deep sense of responsibility to solve some of the problems I'd explored.

14

After my return from the mental health conference, I started to immerse myself in projects. I hooked up with Charles Cochran, who belonged to a group called the Telephone Pioneers of America. Charlie wanted to distribute old teletypewriters that he and his group had reconditioned so that deaf persons could use them. The Pioneers gave me one and asked for my help in finding other people who might be able to use a machine.

I'd never had a way to use the telephone before, and without their help it would have taken much longer. Buying a teletypewriter cost hundreds of dollars, and using one also required another $200 for an acoustic coupler. Tootie Campbell, my friend from the sign language class, talked to the local chapter of Quota Club International, and they agreed to cover the cost of several couplers.

The teletypewriters were real monsters; they took up a lot of space. They also weighed so much that they couldn't be moved easily. Charlie hurt his back taking one from his car to the house of a deaf friend.

I found that many deaf people were not interested in having a teletypewriter. They saw the machines as a luxury because they would be used only to talk to other teletypewriters.

Even after machines were placed in the police department, the hospital, and the library, those three locations were the only ones in our community that could be reached.

Public Law 94-142, then known as the Education for All Handicapped Children Act, had gone into effect. But deaf children were still being taught in public schools with little more support than I'd received. Those who were lucky enough to have classroom interpreters did not necessarily have them for every class. And most of the interpreters had no training in sign language interpreting; they were simply people who'd taken a couple of classes in sign language.

I had endured a lot of what these kids were going through, and I was beginning to realize that much of my success in school happened in spite of, not because of, the system I'd experienced. I couldn't bear watching the kids struggle as I had done.

I tried to help a woman who wanted better services for her deaf daughter. It was tough going because special education programs were still young, and the local school systems weren't used to having to deal with deaf kids. In the past, the kids had been mostly shipped to schools for the deaf, sometimes after they'd dropped hopelessly behind in public schools. The local school system didn't have any professionals who really understood what deafness meant to children.

Besides working at the library full time, and occasionally at the Virginia Book Company, I was also doing freelance writing. I did an article about the horrible conditions at the dog shelter of a nearby county after a friend persuaded me to visit the shelter. The story was printed in the community newspaper, and it generated so much response that the paper hired me to do a follow-up. Occasionally I did public relations work for groups like Shepherd's Ford Center, an idyllic country retreat with offbeat workshops.

Fred and I were playing volleyball a couple of nights each week. We put together a team for league play and won a few tournaments. A regulation-size net was anchored on steel poles in our backyard, and we invited friends to play and practice there. My garden was routinely slaughtered by stray balls.

Toby had trained her pack well. What started as a neat idea, using her to alert me to sounds, had backfired. She was the recognized pack leader, and she took her job as my protector seriously. Tam, Mac, and Leila had copied her behavior to the last twitch and howl. Having one dog bark urgently and come to tell me if someone was at the door was helpful. Having four dogs barking and rushing at me was the cacophony of which nightmares are made. High-strung people left my home tied in knots.

Fred Yates occasionally wrote me letters filled with wisdom and encouragement. In Feburary 1979, his office called me, asking if I could attend a three-day workshop in Williamsburg. Another deaf person had canceled and my name had been suggested as a replacement.

The request came on extremely short notice. I knew little about the focus of the workshop, but I remembered how much I'd learned from the mental health conference. I was eager for more chances to grow. My mother, an avid bridge player, was often asked to substitute for other players at the last minute. Her philosophy was "I should go, because next time I might not get asked." It seemed like a good approach.

The Williamsburg conference was intended to brief persons with disabilities about their rights under Section 504 of the Rehabilitation Act of 1973. This law covered nondiscrimination under federal programs and those supported with federal funds. It had been passed six years earlier, but regulations had been written only recently. Attempts to enforce it had been equally long in coming. The organization giving the workshop, the Public Interest Law Center of Philadelphia, had been a mover and shaker in the disability rights movement.

At the conference, I met persons from all over Virginia who had disabilities, as well as parents and advocates. Over the course of the next few days, they gave me a chance to see what their lives had been like.

The experience was a revelation. Before the conference, I had been on an inward journey, and my focus was on deafness only. I had been absorbed in learning about my disability and searching for ways to help other deaf people.

In Williamsburg I met people with cerebral palsy, epilepsy, spinal cord injuries, learning disabilities, muscular dystrophy, and other labels. They, too, felt anger and frustration because people seemed unwilling to look beyond their disabilities to see their potential. Some of them had been fighting for respect a great deal longer than I had.

I had never seen myself as part of a larger movement, much less a person who had rights that should be protected. The people at the conference became my brothers and sisters. Most of their problems were different from mine, but our barriers all came from the same source. We were up against centuries of ignorance and prejudice.

It was an exhausting conference because of the many tugs at my emotions and the amount of information I was trying to absorb. I was using an interpreter for only the second time; the mental health conference had been my first experience. My sign language vocabulary was still a small one. I was using the lip movements of my sign language interpreters to keep up. My eyes had never had to take so much punishment. I didn't want to miss anything, so I watched lips with a frozen stare.

I quickly realized that I was in the company of an enormous brain trust. The conference attendees with disabilities were some of the brightest people I had ever been exposed to. Yet only a few had jobs that paid a decent wage; fewer still had rewarding jobs that paid well. After three days with them, I knew that I was among people who could do just about anything. The waste of their talents made me furious.

I left the conference a changed and committed person. I was anxious to share the richness of the experience with others. I got in touch with John Chappell and Pat White, two men I had met at the conference. They had helped create a group called Handicaps Unlimited of Virginia, a coalition of persons with disabilities that had several chapters across the state. I thought it would be great to have another one in Winchester.

Through contacts I'd made at the conference, I was also asked to serve on the Advisory Committee of Disabled Individuals, which had been established by the state's Department of Rehabilitative Services to provide consumer input to the agency. The advisory committee's quarterly meetings kept me in touch with a number of the more active disabled persons I'd met in Williamsburg.

Working alongside other persons who had disabilities had changed my view of myself. I was beginning to see how my own behavior shaped the way people looked at me. I was more conscious of how I had become dependent on Fred, allowing him to take care of me in many small ways. He had started to view me in much the same way other people did. But I was helpless in many situations because conditions made me helpless. I wanted to change those conditions.

When I told Fred that I was planning to start a chapter of Handicaps Unlimited, he was very supportive. But when I told him that I wanted to run it because I couldn't find anyone else willing to do so, he cautioned against it. He reminded me that my voice could be difficult for many people to understand, and that I'd need a lot of help running the meetings.

In Williamsburg I had been spent four days with people who had made me feel that there was nothing I couldn't do. I had learned for the first time that it wasn't a sin to ask people to accommodate me. If the people at the conference couldn't understand me, they told me so and we quickly found a way around the problem. They didn't make a big deal out of it or act like it was some kind of major imposition. Our adjustments to meet each other's needs were treated as common courtesy.

That attitude was a radical change for me, since I'd spent more than twenty years adjusting to other people and their needs. I wanted to hold onto the good feelings about myself that I had found in Williamsburg. But that meant that I wanted Fred to treat me the way the Williamsburg people had treated me, and I wanted it yesterday.

Fred knew there was a drastic change in me, but he hadn't gone through the same intense experience. He was confused and upset by my new attitude. It was the first great crisis of our marriage. Happily, we were able to work our way through it over the next few months.

15

My work life began to change. I was no longer participating in the federal job program. My position in the library had become a permanent one and I was earning minimum wage.

I'd had several bad experiences on the job with people who acted as if my deafness was intolerable. Once, a woman had asked me a question that I couldn't speechread. When I'd explained that I was deaf and asked her to repeat the question, she launched into a tirade. The gist of it was that the library had no business employing idiots like me.

A lot of other library users had simply walked away in disgust when I couldn't understand their questions. It had happened often enough that I wasn't anxious to repeat the experience. I sometimes avoided situations in which I knew I might be asked something by a person who did not look friendly.

I knew people raised their eyebrows, tried to make eye contact, and often tilted their heads when they were going to ask a question. During the times I was patching my ego, I would pretend to be very busy if I saw someone approach whose face looked ready to ask something.

I never told the rest of the library staff about my bruising incidents with people who treated me badly. My first supervisor was very perceptive, though, and she noticed that I often seemed awkward in dealing with the public. She tried to encourage me to be less hesitant, but before Williamsburg I couldn't find the courage. I was still struggling when she left to take another job in Connecticut.

My new supervisor, Rosemary Green, arrived as my attitude about myself began to change. She was as much a gem as Anne Lee had been. Rosemary seemed to have total faith in my abilities and she never showed any qualms in delegating work to me. Under her watchful eyes and those of Nancy Harrison, the reference librarian, I developed some of my best coping skills.

Rosemary and Nancy asked me to share some of the reference desk duties so that the library would have good coverage at all times. That kind of work should have had me running for cover, but their confidence in me was strengthening.

I loved reference work. The challenge of finding useful information in a world bombarded daily by new knowledge was equal to anything I'd ever attempted. And every offbeat question gave me a chance to learn something new. Where else could I research how many times lightning strikes the earth each minute and get paid for it?

But the potential for disaster when working at the reference desk was enormous. I would have to deal constantly with adults who talked like Barbara (Her Lips Don't Move, Is She Really Saying Something?) Walters, men with heavy moustaches, and people with dentures. Those types are always difficult to speechread, and things would be even more frenetic because there was no way I could predict what they would ask. When they stood before the reference desk, I was either going to be lucky or dead meat.

My chances for a lucky guess improved when local teachers assigned the same project to an entire class. After I'd helped one or two kids of the same age find the same information, I had more than a vague hunch when another one from that age group approached.

But the first time I did reference work, I knew I was in over my head. There weren't many school kids working on identical projects, and I wasn't guessing lip movements well. I had to ask most people to write their questions for me.

For years, I had used a standard phrase when I couldn't speechread: "I'm sorry, I'm deaf and I didn't understand you. Would you please repeat that?" I discovered that if I was going to survive reference work and hold onto my self-respect, I'd have to change that approach.

I became sick of saying those tired sentences when the questions came fast and furious. I also wasn't getting the desired response. People recoiled in horror when I spoke to them. I was self-conscious about the quality of my "deaf voice," which I had been told was high-pitched. But not all of the questioners were taken aback by for that reason. There were a number of people who wanted information but were embarrassed by their poor writing skills. They'd sooner place a cobra between thumb and forefinger than a pencil.

A lot of people mumbled "that's not important" or "never mind" and left the reference desk when I was in charge. Or they'd write their requests but make it clear that they were irritated by what they considered an imposition.

I seemed to be spending a lot of time apologizing for my deafness. My hearing was gone; that was a given. I didn't need to be hit over the head with the idea that it was a great tragedy or huge affront by everyone who came with a request.

I decided to try another approach and succeeded almost immediately. Humor worked. When a heavily bearded man spoke to me, I'd tease "you want to cut that fur off your face, or grab a pencil and start writing?" If a shy teenage girl hid her lips as she made her request, I'd ask to find out whether her pen-gripping muscles were stronger than my hearing. Just about everything worked better than the old "I'm sorry, I'm deaf, could you write that," approach.

It was a small change, but it brought a great revelation. I discovered that people would, almost without exception, treat me exactly as I expected to be treated. The "I'm sorry" approach set me up to be a pathetic creature, and, sure enough, people talked down to me.

Over time, I improvised and refined my system. And I discovered that it worked as well in the post office or the supermarket as it did in the library. Best of all, as people responded more positively to me, I started to feel better about myself. When I met people with small minds and fast mouths, it was easier to shrug off their hurtful comments.

I started to spend more time with other people who were deaf. I tried to set up a chapter of the Virginia Association of the Deaf, but couldn't quite find enough interested people to keep it going.

Mom and Dad had alluded to the "deaf world" as not being the "real world," and I thought it must be a confining and hopeless place. I kept seeing the phrase "the lonely world of the deaf" in the books and articles I read. But as I made more friends who were deaf, I learned that the deaf world was a community in every sense of the word—one with flaws, but also one with richness. And it was anything but lonely. The people in it were smart, happy, and pretty much like people anywhere else. It was not a terrible place at all.

The irony was that I was condemned to a place far worse, a sort of zombie land. In fact, I had been living there for some time. Hearing people recognized that I was deaf. Deaf people called me "hearing" or "hard of hearing." The labels were different, but they had the same effect. Both held me at arm's length.

Deafness didn't guarantee that I'd be welcomed in the "deaf world." I had never associated with deaf persons before. I knew little about the history or culture of persons who belonged to the Deaf community or their American Sign Language. The signs I had been learning were from a method called Signing Exact English, and they were based on the English language and word order.

I was also considered suspect in the Deaf community because I used a lot of the mannerisms I'd picked up from the hearing people they viewed as their oppressors. When someone who was deaf asked me what the time was, I would sign "quarter to two" instead of responding with the precise "1:48" typical of Deaf culture.

I had bought the myth about sign language—the one that said only quitters and dummies used it. I had often been unhappy, underemployed, and upset. No matter. I was a success because I did not need signs.

I had accepted the myth because everyone around me did. I chattered at people who gave me blank looks and I practiced lip movements endlessly in front of a mirror. Speechreading had given me one source of amusement: it was great for learning choice American curse words while watching sports events on television.

Growing up in the true oralist tradition, I had worked to make the best of my weaknesses instead of relying on my strengths. After I lost my hearing, I had never been able to understand the voice of a single person. But I was forced to try anyway. The oralists had held out the hope that I could, with training, become a crack speechreader and make my voice sound, if not normal, at least unobtrusive. If I couldn't do these things, I was to be a failure for life, doomed to be part of the "deaf world."

It was a devilishly clever approach. All the bases were covered. If my voice wasn't clear or someone seemed to be speaking Chinese, it was always my fault—I was too lazy, inexperienced, not practicing enough, or just plain stupid.

I must have known that no matter what I did, hearing people would still call me deaf. But for eighteen years I had measured deafness in degree. "You don't act deaf" became one of the greatest compliments a hearing person could give me. Although it recognized my deafness, the comment didn't sting. It didn't matter that it implied I was not-as-much-deaf-as-the-others or never-quite-hearing. It was my insurance policy. As long as I could continue to bluff my way through life, I wouldn't be condemned to the "lonely world of the deaf."

On the day I realized I was tired of trying to be what hearing people wanted me to be, I had no comfort. I found that sign language skills alone wouldn't gain me admission to the "deaf world." It was almost more than I could bear. I felt rejected by both worlds, as if no one wanted to claim me.

At the same time, I realized that what I was becoming could be a blessing as well as a curse. There were members of the Deaf community who were kind to me and willing to become my friends. Within the hearing world, I also had friends who sustained me. These people accepted me and cared about me as a person, without conditions. They held out the promise that I could have the best of both worlds.

—————————————16—

As much as I loved the work, I began to realize that my options at Handley Library were very limited. The new addition had opened, and funding had been granted for a children's librarian. I wanted to apply for the position, but I was not encouraged to do so. Although I had worked with children since my first day on the job, I didn't have a master's degree in library science. And I was told that the library wanted a professional for the position.

The person eventually hired had a background largely centered in the publishing of children's books and no degree in library science. She needed some help understanding library systems.

I could see the writing on the wall. I knew that I was appreciated in my job at the library, but I didn't want a job. I wanted a career. I was more than ready for a position with increasing responsibilities and new challenges.

I applied for a public relations position at Shepherd College in nearby West Virginia, which I hoped would put my writing and editing skills to use again. I didn't get the job, but the interviewer contacted me a few weeks later with a hot tip about a weekly newspaper that was trying to get off the ground.

The father and daughter team pulling together the newspaper were not at all put off by my deafness. It helped that the father had lost some of his hearing. After I interviewed, I didn't hear from them for two weeks. When they finally called, they asked me to start work the next day. The position they offered me as assistant editor was far from lucrative, but I knew it would enhance my resume.

I supplemented my income by continuing to work part-time at the library while a search went on for someone to replace me. But the newspaper quickly absorbed my full attention. Since it was a small operation, I had many opportunities to learn new skills.

I had never used a computer before, and I was overwhelmed by the complexity of the Compugraphic typesetting machine that arrived a few weeks after I did. I went to the manufacturer's headquarters for a day of training. I had read part of the manual and played with the machine a little, but I was eager to become more skilled.

The instructor at the training center was called away before he had given more than cursory instructions. I got so bored waiting for him to come back that I started to play with computer commands just to see what they would do. That turned out to be most of my "training," as he spent little time with me and wasn't very helpful anyway. At one point, I asked him a question about one of the functions. He said that it couldn't be used for the task I wanted to accomplish. I simply said "sure it can," and showed him.

When our Compugraphic was delivered to the newspaper office, it still had a lot of bugs to be worked out. We often operated under tight deadlines, and in the West Virginia countryside it was tough to locate a service person when things went wrong. I started to experiment with ways to get the machine to work. I was amazingly successful, and that helped me lose my fear of the computer. In spite of its astounding capabilities, I concluded that I was smarter than the computer because it only knew how to do things one way.

Our newspaper was chronically short of staff. I was asked to do layout and pasteup one week when no one else was available. The publisher was so pleased with my work that she asked me to continue doing it. Then the circulation director was let go and I was asked to assume some of her duties. Eventually I was working as much as sixteen hours a day, including weekends, and the newspaper was becoming my life.

Rosemary Green had persuaded me to take up running when we worked together at Handley Library. I'd tried running with Fred in Newport, but it was humiliating to pant alongside a 6'4" man whose stride was nearly twice the length of mine. I settled for long walks with the dogs and an occasional romp on the beach.

Soon after I started to run with Rosemary, she arranged for a jog around the Winchester hills with Jim Hodson and Ray Gordon. We wanted to learn more about their local group, the Shenandoah Valley Runners. Ray was a retiree, and both he and Jim were in such superb physical condition that I was immediately sold on the health benefits of running.

The newspaper office was located near a national park, which gave me a perfect place to take running breaks. I was home so little that I started bringing the dogs to work with me, and we all got our exercise during my runs. Fred took to stopping by whenever he was visiting a physician in West Virginia on sales calls.

On one occasion, when Fred and I were walking the dogs through the park, our youngest, Leila, was caught in a rusted metal trap. We had never anticipated finding traps on federal park land, and I'd walked through the area many times without incident. Before we could free her, Leila bit through several fingers on my right hand. It was a frightening experience. I had no idea how those contraptions worked, and she was so crazed with fright that we could barely restrain her long enough to spring the trap.

I was so concerned about the newspaper deadline that as soon as we had informed the park officials and made sure that Leila would be all right, I went straight back to work for several hours. My hand had started to swell alarmingly. I knew that if I didn't finish typing the next issue before my fingers became stiff and painful, I would be unable to meet the deadline.

I was deliriously happy at the newspaper, but I was also chronically short of sleep. I started to have a succession of strange viruses. I knew I couldn't keep up the fast pace and long hours forever. I was especially upset after I was pressed into service to take over for a reporter who kept missing deadlines. It was heady to write stories and take pictures. But among my new duties was that of bookkeeping. And I discovered that the reporter was being paid regularly each week, while my checks were sporadic. I felt very much taken advantage of, not only because I had started bailing out the reporter by doing her work, but also because she was being paid far more than I was.

I decided to talk with the publishing team. The daughter agreed to have lunch with me, during which I outlined some of my concerns. I reminded her of our original contract and told her that my hours needed to be reduced. I asked for the same salary as the reporter. She agreed to think over my request and call to leave a message with Fred in the morning about her decision. The next day was a Saturday; we did not hear from her the entire weekend.

I did not want to go to work over the weekend without knowing what the conditions would be, even though I knew it would be tough to get out the next issue of the newspaper. So, on Monday, I drove to the office. The front desk person, who was very new, acted surprised to see me. I went to my work area and saw that all the articles I had been working on for the next issue were gone. I was stunned. I found my clock and other personal items stuck in a box in the back room. Not knowing what else to do, I grabbed the box, drove home, and cried.

I had put my heart into that job, night and day. Suddenly I had nothing to do. Fred's work with Pfizer could keep us comfortable without my additional income, small as it was. But like someone who has fallen from a horse and has to remount, I needed desperately to work. A friend helped me find a temporary job working nights at the local hospital, entering medical records into a computer. I also had some part-time work at the library to fall back on.

Although I was so devastated by the experience that I vowed never to work for anyone again, the newspaper had at least done me one big favor—after eight years outside my chosen field, I had confidence in my writing and editing skills again. In anticipation of free time I'd never found, I had set up a public relations business when I started at the newspaper. I decided to see if I could make a go of it in Winchester.

I talked with a graphic artist who occasionally referred editing jobs to me. I had business cards printed up, and I mailed them with a cover letter to several area businesses.

Luck was on my side. The town's Chevrolet-Cadillac dealership was changing hands. The new owner, Jim Stutzman, was looking for a public relations person when my letter came across his desk. He asked me to stop by.

We talked about his goals for the dealership. Jim felt that if he was fair to everyone and offered good services, people would come to trust him and give him their business. He disliked the misleading advertisements used by some other car dealers he had known, and he refused to adopt their approach. Could I work with that kind of philosophy, he asked. You bet I could.

Jim Stutzman Chevrolet-Cadillac became my first major client, and within weeks I was designing print advertisements and radio spots and ghostwriting Jim's weekly newspaper column. The radio spots were a bit troublesome at first—I'd never heard one. But I got some wonderful coaching from Roy Nester, a kind and talented man who worked for WINC radio.

Now that I was able to be home more, I was anxious to get my chapter of Handicaps Unlimited off the ground. I threw my public relations skills into recruiting people, setting up meetings, and getting the word out. The exposure led to my being asked to serve on the Special Education Advisory Committee for Winchester's schools and the city's Equal Employment Opportunity Commission.

I was also becoming more active in projects at the state level. I took over chairing the public relations committee for the state organization, Handicaps Unlimited of Virginia, and soon was elected vice president of the group.

Fred was beginning to work with me in the disability rights movement, and as he became exposed to the people I'd met at Williamsburg, he was infected with the same zeal to change the world. He was a great sounding board, and he played devil's advocate with relish. Fred was a great asset because he listened to the arguments of people who didn't understand disability and repeated them to me in a way that forced me to hone my responses.

I learned from my work with Handicaps Unlimited that not every person with a disability was enthusiastic about making the world free of barriers. It seemed that there were two distinct groups: fighters who struggled to achieve and people who accepted what was dished out, trying to make the best of it.

I was definitely one of the fighters. My group made up in brass and loudness what we lacked in numbers.

I came to understand that the people who did nothing had many reasons for their inertia—fear, ignorance, and sometimes simple tiredness or lack of time. What I found hardest to comprehend was that some did not even know how to dream.

I knew how dreams could die. I had a harder time figuring out why people had no hope. Over the years, I had started to sound like a cynic, but my pessimistic air was camouflage. Having experienced so many setbacks and disappointments, it was easier for me to expect the worst. Then, if things didn't turn out badly, I had something to celebrate.

As I looked more closely at my friends who were complacent, I started to understand how important their parents had been in shaping their views of themselves. The words and actions of mothers and fathers had become firmly ingrained. Some people whose parents had negative views of them because of their disabilities eventually became enlightened and learned to challenge those views. But not many. The parents who couldn't overcome the impulse to protect a child often raised kids who felt helpless and didn't know how to make decisions. People who had been placed in institutions or sent away to school often had the worst of it. They'd never really had parents in the true sense, only caretakers.

I discovered that I had been lucky to have parents who pushed me. For years, because they often pushed before I was ready, I thought Mom and Dad didn't love me. I had viewed the dances they made me attend and the other things they forced me to do as punishments. But as much as I hated the prodding, I had to admit that one thing came across loud and clear. No matter what I did, my parents expected a lot from me. I felt that they knew I hadn't done my best work yet.

17

Some of the best fighters I met in the disability rights movement didn't have to worry about their parents' perception of them, or anyone else's. People who became disabled later in life often had already developed an identity or two, such as worker, spouse, or parent, before disability came along and changed everything. They didn't take kindly to being relegated to a second-class role.

I began to find it humorous that so many people couldn't accept themselves as persons with disabilities, at least when I wasn't depressed about it. These folks seemed to think that disabilities were what happened to other people. They'd say "I don't consider myself disabled" and give some excuse about why they were different.

When disabilities happened to people, their lives were changed in ways they could never predict. Good looks and a family with wealth or a well-known name provided insulation for a few. Money might not buy happiness, but it certainly could help command respect and buy the best of adaptations, therapy, training, and equipment.

I was continuing to learn new signs from the deaf people I met in Winchester. Marshall and Mildred Butler had visited the library regularly with their hearing daughter, Martha, while I worked there. They were patient with me as I struggled to remember my sign language vocabulary, and they urged me to come to services at their church. The Winchester Deaf Fellowship had been meeting for over twenty years in space donated by the Church of the Brethren. Eight to ten Sundays each year, if Mother Nature cooperated, there were services for the deaf fellowship, followed by potluck dinners.

Fred and I attended a service. Fred actually understood more of what was happening than I did because a volunteer voiced an interpretation of the signs for him. My ability to read signs was still too limited to be dependable, but I was taken by the cheerful fellowship and grateful for the warmth with which I was welcomed.

Watching the preacher, Warren Blackwell, I saw the Bible come to life through sign language. His sermons were magnificent theater as well as profound teaching. The grace and power of sign language were a perfect match for religious instruction, and I was not surprised to find out later that the roots of American Sign Language could be traced to religious people who brought a language of signs from France. After witnessing the extraordinary beauty of the deaf fellowship's services, I found hearing churches bland by comparison.

The deaf people who belonged to the Winchester Deaf Fellowship came from many different backgrounds. Few belonged to the Brethren church. They had been raised as Baptists, Lutherans, Catholics, and many other denominations.

I was comfortable with this mix of backgrounds because of my past experiences. Mom and Dad had been members of Gram and Gramp McIntosh's Episcopal church before we moved to Pennsylvania. The closest Episcopal church was a half hour's drive from Woolrich. My parents liked the warmth of the local Methodist church, so they decided to join. They had always treated the beliefs of others with respect and tolerance.

At Woolrich Community Church, I'd gone to Sunday school and church services every week until I left for college.

Dad was a lay preacher and also taught Sunday school. Mom was active on several church committees. I'd learned the comfort of shared traditions. We sang the same refrain when collecting the offering, and we always recited the Apostle's Creed during the service. I loved the deep rumble of vibrations in the old wood pews when people would speak or sing in unison.

My parents sat directly below the minister's podium every Sunday, but I'd never been able to understand anything the minister said. I was restless and daydreamed a lot during the service, unless David spiced things up. He wasn't above threatening me with a straight pin taken from the ribbons reserved for visitors. Most of the time, though, I tried to look interested and stare at the minister while lost in the worlds created by my imagination.

Sunday school and Bible school had been just as boring for me. I was happiest at the beginning of the year, when the new Sunday school textbooks came and gave me something to read.

In college, I learned that there were saints and sinners of every faith. During my freshman year, I mentioned this observation to my resident assistant. She was involved in a group called "Way Out Worship," W.O.W. for short. She invited me to join her for some meetings, and I ended up becoming a member of the group.

We were about a dozen people of different faiths trying to find a way to reach out to each other in a generic-yet-profound fashion. Our methods were atypical. I worked with others to create a dance to "Bridge Over Troubled Water" as part of our service. I like breaking new ground and using dance to contribute to the religious experience. But with W.O.W., as at Woolrich Community Church, I did not get anything back. I couldn't speechread most of the people at our meetings, and they were too busy to invest time in friendships when the meetings ended. I drifted away from the group after a couple of months.

By the time I left college, I had the beginnings of a very private but very intense faith. I'd taken a course in religious studies, in which I'd been fascinated by the similarities and differences in major religions.

I'd seen a lot of "Sunday Christians" who were lousy people all week but seemed to think they could behave that way as long as they went to church on Sunday. I'd had my first run-in with fanatics from a group called Campus Crusade for Christ. I had made mistakes by being judgmental, and I wasn't proud of my reactions.

After we moved to Winchester, Fred had to contend with another problem. He was buttonholed by neighbors who thought he should bring me to a faith healer. Neither of us took kindly to the idea that I was automatically considered a sinner because I couldn't hear.

One day, on my return from a trip to Richmond, I found a man and woman waiting with Fred in our living room. The woman told me she lived in New York and that she'd had a dream about me. Soon after the dream, she flew to Norfolk. Arriving at the airport, she happened to pick up a newspaper, and there she found a picture of me with a story written by my college friend, Julie Dunlap. She recognized me as the person from her dream.

The woman had decided that it was her mission to find me, so she walked to a line of cabs outside the airport. She claimed that some impulse told her to choose the third one. The man with her now had been the driver of the cab. After hearing her story, he had driven her five hours to see me.

I was flabbergasted. The woman seemed to know a lot about me. I didn't know whether she had picked up details from talking to Fred or from the newspaper article, but it was still spooky. She and the driver were African Americans. I couldn't imagine two people going to so much trouble unless the message was important.

To them, it was. If I accepted Jesus and became born again, the woman told me, my hearing would return.

They asked that Fred and I join hands in prayer with them. We obliged. They refused my offer to put them up for the night, although it was very late. They left behind a flyer about "Jews for Jesus" and never contacted me again.

When I tried to make sense of the experience, everything got mixed up. I was totally put off by the requirement that I be "born again" to get my hearing back. My faith had been tested and it was a strong one. I felt it would be a sham to pretend to lose God so that I could "find" him on the hope that I would hear again.

I didn't sleep much that night, or for many nights after that. While thinking about the incident, I was stunned to realize that after all the years of learning to cope with the limitations people placed on me, functioning as a deaf person was all I knew how to do. Imagining a world in which, suddenly, everything would be within reach was overwhelming and actually frightening. Although the reward of hearing was tempting, what I really wanted most was not to hear but to find fairness and understanding.

18

Tootie Campbell, my signing friend, encouraged me to join Quota Club. The members of Quota were women who either owned a business or held executive positions in a company. I was attracted by the club's commitment to provide funding to support services for persons with hearing loss. Quota Club had helped to get those first teletypewriters placed in Winchester.

Tootie and I found that we celebrated our birthdays a week apart in October, though I was a year older. We started a tradition of throwing ourselves a party. We also enjoyed planning a prank each year for Quota Club's district conference. Among our favorites was a "discovery" of the true history of Quota, in which we revealed that the original motto was "so many men, so little time."

Quota Club was very special to me. It gave me the first opportunity I'd ever had to be a valued part of a group of professionals. The members of Quota made an outstanding effort to include me and use my skills. They set aside hundreds of dollars each year to provide sign language interpreters so that I could participate in their meetings.

Fred joined the local Jaycees. We had long been volunteering each other for favorite projects, and he recruited me to help with the Jaycees' annual Halloween Haunted House fundraiser.

We had a great time dressing in macabre costumes. With Fred's height and his convincing attempt to look menacing, he made a magnificent henchman. I was drafted to be the hapless woman cut up by the mad doctor with the chain saw. It was the perfect excuse to scream my lungs out. My only concern was that the Scream Queen role might become what people most remembered about me, just as Mr. Barry never tired of the story about my tooth retainer.

Although Gramp McIntosh had been a politician, I was suspicious and distrustful of most elected officials. As I became more active in the disability rights movement, I realized it might be much easier to change misguided government policies from the inside.

Fred and I had always voted for the person whose goals and commitment we liked, not for a party. We had friends on both ends of the political spectrum and everywhere in between. We were uncertain about which political party to work with.

Ira Lechner solved our problem. After we heard him speak at a Handicaps Unlimited conference, we felt we had found a person who could prove that "honest politician" did not have to be an oxymoron. We became Democrats to help him get elected. Ira's bid was unsuccessful, but one thing led to another. Within a few years, Fred became chairman of the local party. I may not have been the first deaf person to be a delegate to the state Democratic Party convention, but I apparently introduced most of the other delegates to the use of a sign language interpreter.

I took a day trip to Gallaudet College to study Cued Speech with associates of Dr. Owen Cornett, the founder of the method. Although cued speech had been in use for almost two decades, few people knew what it was. Most of the deaf people I talked to had derogatory things to say about it. They called it "crude speech" or "cute speech."

I tried to memorize the simple cueing hand shapes and positions, which were based on phonetics, but quickly decided to focus on sign language instead. My brain absorbed language based not on the way words sounded but the way they were spelled. I found cueing to be an uncomfortable disruption of my thought process.

I could have changed my mindset with a little tenacity. Cued speech could have helped me speechread with the same accuracy as sign language. My pronunciation of unfamiliar words might have improved. But sign language beckoned me with an unbeatable benefit. It offered access to a language used by many thousands more people—people with a history and a culture. There were some people who signed in Winchester, but practically no one knew how to cue.

Life came full circle for me. Within three years after the fateful conference in Williamsburg, I had contracted with Barrier Free Environments, in Raleigh, N.C., to serve as a trainer for their workshops on Section 504 in various cities along the Eastern Seaboard. It was the most fulfilling work I had ever done. I watched other people with disabilities grow as I had done in Williamsburg. I felt enormously privileged to be part of their growth. Phil Calkins and Linda Field Miller, the workshop leaders, were outstanding planners and human rights activists. I watched them and tried to copy their ability to pull the best from people. They introduced me to the works of Si Kahn, from which I learned solid principles of organizing. And they told me about the Highlander Folk School, which had played a strong role in the birth of the labor unions and the civil rights movement.

Linda gave me a copy of *Unearthing Seeds of Fire*, which chronicled the odyssey of Myles Horton, founder of the Highlander School. As I read about his principles, I learned priceless rules about teaching and sustaining movements. Horton searched for the secret of education because he understood instinctively that much of what passed for teaching failed to connect with people's lives. He learned two fundamental things:

that people know the answers to their problems, and that the teacher's job is to get them talking about their problems, to raise and sharpen questions, and to trust people to come up with the answers. Highlander School also did not disdain the idea of creative conflict as a means to social change. And Horton discovered that teachers taught not so much by their teaching but by their capacity to learn.

The Highlander School was so successful at promoting social change through its focus on labor and race relations that its enemies tried to destroy it. After an injunction closed the school, Horton said, "You can padlock a building, but you can't padlock an idea. Highlander is an idea. You can't kill it, and you can't close it in . . . it will grow wherever people take it."

The disability rights movement had enlarged my focus, but I still had more growing to do. I came to realize that everything I had been doing was tied into a much larger struggle for human rights. This led to my involvement with organizations like Amnesty International. I believed that every human being had the right to be treated with respect and dignity, and those who would infringe on that right could never be tolerated.

Activism was becoming my way of life. I had been named to the Governor's Overall Advisory Council on Needs of Handicapped Persons. I was Vice Chair of the Advisory Committee for Disabled Individuals, which advised the state's Department of Rehabilitative Services. I became the Chair when the incumbent died suddenly.

I was heavily involved in my Handicaps Unlimited chapter, and just as involved at the state level. In 1982, I was elected president of the state organization, and in the three months following my election, I put more than 3,000 miles on my car with trips to Richmond and elsewhere. Travel by car was never one of my favorite pastimes because I liked to do at least two things at a time. But with my hearing loss I couldn't listen to the radio or tapes as I drove. My trips were only bearable because I had found the world's best traveling companion.

Angie Papke had moved back to Winchester from Charlottesville, after health problems prevented her from working. She had osteogenesis imperfecta, which had resulted in a hearing loss as well as making it impossible for her to walk without support. Angie came to a meeting of my Handicaps Unlimited chapter, and within weeks we were fast friends. Angie not only knew signs, but she also was a *summa cum laude* graduate of the school of hard knocks.

In June 1982, I participated in the first Access to Equality Conference. The conference was an attempt to bring together leaders in the movements for quality education, women's rights, and disability rights.

We talked about statistics. For every dollar a white male made, women were earning $.59 by comparison. But a white woman with a disability earned $.35 and a black woman with a disability earned just $.12. It was clear that women with disabilities had far to go.

I served as one of the three facilitators for the disability rights track at the conference. My group discussed research that showed how men saw themselves as men first and disabled second. By contrast, women often identified themselves as disabled first and women second. We also talked about how important it was to have role models. Some of the disabled women at the conference said that when they were young, they didn't know what they had to look forward to. One said that because she knew no adults with her disability, she thought she'd outgrow it.

Her words reminded me of my own confusion after I became deaf. I remembered seeing the "Today Show" on television and feeling kinship with the anchors. I thought they were wearing hearing aids. I didn't understand why I couldn't grow up to be a newscaster like Dave Garroway.

I wasn't good at saying no, so I served on a lot of commissions and committees. I vowed never to be a token deaf person. If I chose to commit myself to something, I did more than show up at meetings. When the Department of Rehabilitative Services asked me to serve on a committee to look at the agency's need for better public relations, I accepted. Then I told them the truth: they couldn't use their small public relations staff as a scapegoat for the negative view consumers had of their agency. All the employees from top to bottom needed to recognize that they were responsible for the department's image. No amount of slick packaging could solve their problems if the people working in the agency were hampered by poor policies or if they were incompetent.

I was doing prodigious amounts of public relations work, but 90 percent of my time was spent on volunteer projects, not with paying clients. I was fortunate to have a husband who was supporting me in every possible way.

It was a challenging time to be involved in disability rights. The independent living movement had come to Virginia, and Handicaps Unlimited's state organization was to be a partner in the creation of the first independent living center in Norfolk. At the same time, the rights gained under Section 504 and under Public Law 94-142 were under attack by the new president, Ronald Reagan, and his administration.

I drove to Washington and Philadelphia to plead with officials from the Department of Education not to jettison P.L. 94-142. I argued that the law needed to be fine tuned, but not junked.

At the Washington hearing, I told officials about a deaf man I'd met. He was an extremely bright student who had just graduated from a high school in which he'd been mainstreamed. He'd managed to succeed largely because he'd taken a tape recorder to school and recorded his classes. Every afternoon and evening, his mother had listened to the tapes and transcribed every lecture and class discussion. I found his story mind-boggling. I hoped the officials would be appalled but would understand that deaf children could succeed in school if they had support. While the attention had paid off for this man, not many kids had a mother who could give that kind of dedication.

I also spent some time on Capitol Hill, where I met with a group of people trying to ensure that Section 504 would be preserved. We had strategy sessions and met with members of Congress to share our concerns. I was relieved when our work and that of others resulted in both laws surviving intact.

I was one of the first persons to buy a closed caption decoder, placing an order at Sears well in advance of the sale date. I couldn't wait to figure out my husband's attraction to television. As a child, I'd enjoyed shows where the antics were highly visual, especially those with comics such as Carol Burnett, Jackie Gleason, and Red Skelton. Sometimes I used dramatic programs to fuel my fantasy life; I made up the story as I watched.

Fred was a fan of "Hill Street Blues" and "Barney Miller." Both shows were memorable for great dialogue, which I couldn't appreciate.

When I brought my decoder home, "Hill Street" wasn't captioned, but "Barney Miller" was. The first show I watched was a rerun, so Fred wasn't interested in viewing it with me. He went to work on a project in the basement. Shortly after he went downstairs, he heard me screaming and came to investigate. He found me in front of the television, bent nearly double from laughing too hard.

We were delighted to find something that we could enjoy doing together. I became so hooked on captioned television shows that I refused to watch anything that wasn't captioned. I also wasn't interested in seeing any more movies in theaters; I would wait until they came out on videotape and say prayers that they'd be distributed with captions. *Star Wars* was the last movie I saw on the big screen.

19

As I became more skilled at sign language, I switched from using oral transliterators to using sign language transliterators, or sign language interpreters as they were more commonly known.

During the years I was trying to blend in, I hadn't used interpreters. Sign language interpreting was still relatively new as a profession.

My first oral transliterators were a great help. They sat a couple of feet in front of me and simply repeated what was being said. When I couldn't find someone with training as an oral transliterator, I'd draft anyone whom I could speechread well, including Fred. By focusing on one person whose face was well lit and who stayed in the same place, my understanding of what was happening really improved.

However, I learned quickly that husbands are not a good choice for that kind of work. It is very tiring to have to keep listening, processing information, and passing it on. The temptation to start selecting information instead of repeating it all was tremendous, especially for people doing the tedious work for free.

I started to switch to sign language interpreters who were easy to speechread and who mouthed words as they signed them. I was astonished to discover how much difference it made. I was more relaxed because, between the signs and the speechreading, I could follow conversations almost perfectly. If I didn't understand a word on the lips, the sign gave me a second chance.

In fact, sign language interpreters were so liberating that when I went back to using oral interpreters, I noticed how quickly I became tired and how much more often I was baffled. I also noticed that the things I saw on the lips didn't sink in. A couple of hours or days after a meeting, what I'd seen on the lips would all come together in my brain. That was when I wanted to kick myself for not asking more questions at the meetings.

The biggest revelation occurred on those occasions when I went to meetings with no interpreters at all. I could barely understand a thing. I was beginning to realize that I had been kidding myself for years. And I was appalled at how much I had missed.

The more I served on boards and commissions, the more skills I learned for surviving meetings. I got better at telling people what would help me be a good participant.

Still, it was tricky. I had a habit of cutting off speakers, not because I was rude but because I couldn't always figure out when to jump in on a discussion. My interpreters repeated what they heard, and they were always a sentence or two behind the last speaker. I tried to find out who was talking and watch for that person to finish, but sometimes another person jumped in before I could.

I saw plenty of meetings deteriorate into chaos as people cut in on each other because they didn't ask for recognition before speaking. I became familiar with the wild-eyed look interpreters wore when several people talked at once, and I would watch them try to decide which speaker to interpret. Most of them confessed that they chose to interpret the person talking the loudest.

After I had used my first professionally trained interpreters, I was spoiled forever. Pat Isaacs was a jewel. One of the first times I used her, we arrived at a social event, and she gave me a choice I'd never had before. Without being asked, she worked rapid-fire, interpreting snatches of several conversations so that I could decide which one I wanted to join.

Later, at a more formal meeting, I saw one hand dart over her head, shaped in the sign that signifies an airplane. While she made the sign, she kept interpreting the speaker's conversation with her other hand. Because the airplane sign had nothing to do with the context of what she'd been signing, it caught me off balance. The third time she used the airplane sign, comprehension dawned. Our conference room was located next to a naval air base. Pat was letting me know when planes passing overhead drowned out the speaker's voice.

Ellen Trimble was another interpreter who won my respect for "above-and-beyond" performance. I barely knew her when she was called on to interpret a telephone conversation for me. Hugging the telephone receiver between ear and shoulder, she started to sign. I was distracted by what seemed to be a facial tic. While she signed, her eyes kept narrowing as if she wanted to squint. After several minutes of first-rate interpreting, the call was completed. As Ellen removed the receiver from her ear, I realized what had caused her to wince. The telephone was outfitted with an amplifier, and she had been wincing in pain because the volume was turned up. She was too professional to interrupt the conversation or stop interpreting long enough to turn it down.

Paige Berry was in a class by herself. At one conference I attended, a band was providing entertainment. Paige signed some terrific songs for me and the other deaf persons at my table. The most remarkable thing about her performance was that the band music she interpreted had no words. She was making up the lyrics as she went along.

I used Jan Nishimura as an oral interpreter when I didn't

know signs. She was great. After I knew signs, I used her to transliterate. She was great. Then I watched her interpret for friends using American Sign Language. She was still great. A Triple Threat Woman—truly amazing.

Jan Bailey, the founder of Sign Language Associates, introduced me to the magic of performance interpreting. I saw her interpret *The Sound of Music* and was in awe. While she signed, she projected the Von Trapp children so well that each personality was clearly recognizable.

I could work for long periods at a high level of intensity except when speechreading was involved. It sapped my energy like a chronic case of jet lag.

As I learned more about the mysteries of the brain, I found out why that happened. Using my senses gave a workout to my brain cells. I had 75 to 100 trillion cells constantly analyzing, sending, and receiving messages. Of all the senses, vision is the biggest user of cells, much more so than hearing. My brain cells got more exercise than a hearing person's because I depended on my eyes for most of my information.

When I understood that, I finally realized why I got so exhausted on the first day of school or at parties with strange people. There was so much to soak up and make sense of! My days were so routinely exhausting that I had been one of the few children who went to bed without complaint.

Sometimes I just couldn't handle all the information my eyes sent to my brain to sort out. I called these overdoses of visual information "blitzing out." Like a malfunction in a pinball machine, where something sticks and the lights and sound effects keep repeating, my brain would give up and send out the message "does not compute."

I tried to learn eye pollution control, but it was impossible. My all-time award for cruel and unusual punishment went to a hotel that mirrored the entire ceiling of its huge conference room. I spent two days feeling crazed. I tried to watch my interpreter, but my eyes caught every movement in the room as it was reflected overhead—hands reaching for a water pitcher, people scribbling notes, tissues dabbing noses.

I was like a person who, once having tasted freedom, could never give it up. Fred had kept up with my changes. I'd taught him some of what I was learning in my sign language classes. When I couldn't understand what he was saying, he would repeat it with signs and fingerspelling. My home had become my safe place. With Fred, I had no secrets and no barriers to communication.

Outside our house, though, things were very different. I was finding that visits with others in my family left me tense, drained, and sometimes ill.

Gayle had a husband and kids, Randy had married, and Dave had girlfriends. I was trying to deal with a family twice the size it had been.

I was very conscious of what I was missing. My family was a collection of screwballs, all Type A personalities, and our get-togethers were frenetic. I especially hated mealtimes. Scintillating talk flew around the table and I wanted very much to be part of the discussion. The topics interested me.

I wanted to make the perfectly timed smart remark that would crack everyone up. I wanted to share all the knowledge I'd amassed and lead discussions down tantalizing avenues. I wanted to stop feeling like a stranger.

Fred and I felt very inhibited when we signed around my parents. They were proud of my speechreading and speaking abilities, and they made me feel that signing was almost an insult to them.

I had learned from other people with disabilities that family members often took for granted or overlooked each other's needs. If we didn't like their behavior, we were stuck. We couldn't divorce them or rip out our genes.

I had two friends who used wheelchairs. One had been forced to ask for help from her family for thirty years because her parents' home had a bathroom she was unable to use. Yet her folks could well afford the inexpensive modifications that would have made her independent.

My other friend's family had a house with no ramps to any of the doors. She couldn't go in or out without "asking permission," since someone would have to carry her up and down the steps.

I had always been close to my family, but I was beginning to dread my time with them as much as I looked forward to it. I tried for a couple of years to run from the problem, avoiding most get-togethers or cutting them short. I was good at finding excuses. I had plenty of projects to keep me busy.

20

I was concerned about the quality of health care for persons with disabilities. There were doctors and nurses who treated me like a perpetual patient although only one part of me was out of order. From my friends who had disabilities, I learned about surgery that was ostensibly being done to correct a condition but actually amounted to little more than experimentation on human patients. A paraplegic woman told me she'd had to teach her own doctor how to deliver her baby. And I met other people with disabilities who were being drugged into oblivion.

These experiences and many others led me to become active in the National Women's Health Network, where I tried to bring some focus to the concerns of women with disabilities. Through the Network, I met Judy Norsigian of the Boston Women's Health Collective, one of the authors of *Our Bodies, Ourselves*. Judy, in turn, introduced me to Irving Kenneth Zola, a professor at Brandeis University.

Irv became disabled as a result of polio when he was younger. He taught me, through his example, to be more careful in my choice of words. I had unquestioningly accepted many of the terms and labels used by persons who had no personal experience with disability. One of the great offenders was "overcoming a disability." Reporters used the phrase to describe persons whose actions were not necessarily heroic but whose feats must have seemed amazing to someone who had never had to face the constant adversity that went hand-in-hand with some disabilities. Sometimes the action that these writers praised amounted to little more than an extraordinary attempt at denial of a disability. I was often praised for my outstanding speechreading abilities. Other people I knew were lauded because they were determined to struggle with crutches rather than "give up" and use wheelchairs. My more sensible wheelchair-using friends told me they'd rather save their time and energy for their work than lose it all climbing stairs and hiking to restrooms.

Irv had written about disability-related topics for years and had dedicated himself to learning how to cope as best he could. He knew that no matter how great his skill at coping, his disability would never go away. He saw adjusting as a lifelong process. I admired his outlook and patterned my thinking after his.

My friend Carolyn White Hodgins, then director of the Office for the Developmentally Disabled, cut to the heart of the matter when she pointed out that "disability doesn't automatically make someone more noble." We all knew people who were pretty poor human beings both before and after they became disabled.

Trying to bring about changes in Winchester and the surrounding area was difficult for me. My parents had raised me to be polite; though, like them, I could be stubborn when I was stepped on. I thought that I would only have to appeal to the nobler instincts in people, explaining what was needed and why it was important. But I found that all my public relations skills didn't matter as much as the almighty dollar.

I never understood how something that would bring fairness and much-needed respect to people could cost too much. I hated the numbers games. Whenever I would ask for the entrance of a building to be ramped or for a TDD to be added to an office, someone always wanted to know how many people would benefit. That question made no sense to me. I thought everyone had value, and helping one person was goal enough. I saw the changes as more of an investment than an expense.

One of the biggest struggles I had was in learning to like myself as an advocate. I made enemies of people who wanted to do nothing to change their unfair and discriminatory practices. I hated being viewed as a hard-nosed bitch when I visited the local hospital and asked for improvements to services that were already required by law. But I didn't hate it enough to abandon my principles and stop fighting. Politeness, I discovered, had its limitations.

For a long time, I wondered what was wrong with me. I'd push fruitlessly for changes such as Brailled materials, raised numbers on elevators, electric doors, and interpreter services. Then someone who knew nothing about my fight would politely make the same request and get it granted.

Sometimes I'd hear about the success when the lucky person bragged about how responsive people had been. I'd wonder if we could possibly be talking about the same people. I had asked nicely the first time I made the request, too, and it got me nowhere. So I tried other forms of persuasion that weren't so polite.

Then I got an education about the "good guy, bad guy" approach, also known as "good cop, bad cop." I found that the ploy was being used very successfully in other parts of Virginia, especially by John Chappell and Pat White, who were leaders in Handicaps Unlimited. The bad guy would go somewhere and raise hackles by telling folks they were breaking the law and threatening dire consequences if the sun and moon were not delivered pronto, with gift wrap. After everybody's blood pressure was nicely on the upswing, the good guy would come along. Good guy didn't put much emphasis on lawsuits or quote passages of antidiscrimination law. Simple, heartfelt, and humble pitches were the good guy's forte.

It was a great formula. The good guy would end up getting everything that the bad guy wanted. Because the good guy seemed reasonable and in need of sympathy, he was a fellow people could relate to because he reinforced stereotypes. He didn't raise the guilt level in folks who hadn't been doing the right thing. He let them feel they were doing a favor, not reminding them of something they ought to have been doing in the first place.

My mental health was better when I understood that, unintentionally, I had been forced into a perpetual bad guy role. I was providing an important service. I started to have a gag reflex whenever I heard people say "you can catch more flies with honey than with vinegar." Many times I found that the careful groundwork laid by persons willing to play the bad guy was what made it possible for others to reap the dividends. I developed deep appreciation for the bad guy types because, although they were the catalysts for change, they made few friends and rarely got credit.

Trying to break people of the caretaker habit was another great challenge I faced. My friends and I would convince people to make modifications to improve accessibility, only to see our hard work backfire when they tried to make a grand gesture or surprise us.

Instead of asking us what we wanted and involving us in making changes, they'd put in ramps that were too steep, restrooms with entrances that were too narrow, and TDDs that were incompatible with others or too complicated for infrequent users to learn. They were upset when their efforts met with criticism instead of praise. Sometimes they'd complain about the huge cost involved, when we could have saved them a great deal of money if they'd asked us for input.

I was becoming the scribe of Winchester. It seemed that whatever group Fred or I became involved in, from the dog training club to the Democrats, I ended up doing their newsletter. At my peak, I was churning out newsletters for four groups each month. Virtually all my writing and editing of newsletters was for nonprofit groups, and I was adept at finding ways to keep costs low. I was on good terms with printers, and I invested in a second personal computer so that I could do all the typesetting, paste-up, and layout at home.

In 1983, Fred and I bought an old house on Washington Street, which we set about restoring bit by bit. We added a garage, a laundry room, a kitchen addition, and a workshop. With four bedrooms—or seven, if we reclaimed rooms from other uses—there was plenty of space for visitors and entertaining. Both sets of parents fell for the house's charm as quickly as we had. Mom and Dad McIntosh visited several times to help us paint and do other projects. Mom even brought a friend, Florence Edwards, to help sew drapes for my dining room.

Our Washington Street home enabled me to keep running from my problems even more effectively. I was at ease on my new turf. I could occupy every minute with things that made me comfortable.

Family get-togethers were a lot of fun, especially during the annual Apple Blossom Festival. My parents; Fred's parents; Gram Webber; my siblings and their husbands, wives, or significant others, and sometimes their friends, would fill the house with laughter. The festival, held every spring, had major events for four days and not one, but two, long parades. Our house had a long front yard overlooking the parade route, and we reserved the sidewalk area for our neighbors and their friends.

Everyone in my family arrived for the festival bearing food—too much of it. I'd continue having parties after the festival ended just to clean out my pantry and two refrigerators.

I loved to have company. I could fuss with flower arrangements, make my most sinful desserts, and create beautiful table settings. Refilling coffee cups and checking casseroles in the oven gave me the perfect excuse to avoid struggling with conversations I couldn't follow easily. Making a good time for everyone else kept me from being obsessed by the emptiness I was feeling.

21

I'd left my darkroom behind when we moved to Washington Street. It was no great tragedy because I had little spare time to dabble in photography. I had another hobby, collecting teddy bears. In one of the guest bedrooms, which we called the "Bear Room," they sprawled on every piece of furniture. The bears were special to me because of the stories attached to them or the people who gave them to me.

Fred humored me by commemorating memorable events with additions to the bear collection. After a couple of years, out of curiosity, I started to design and sew my own bears. Fred made wood joints for them in his workshop and was a master at installing eyes. On cold winter nights, as we watched our favorite programs on television, we would put stuffing in the bodies.

I taught some community sign language classes as a fundraiser for the Handicaps Unlimited chapter. It was fun to introduce people to signs. I wanted to make them as enthusiastic about signing as I was.

Not long after I started teaching, Shenandoah College contacted me to ask if I would be interested in instructing their students. I wasn't eager for more work, but the college was having difficulty finding a replacement for its previous instructor. I was always a sucker for anyone in need.

My first college class was full of the kind of bright, eager kids who made teaching a pleasure. I had fun coming up with new ways to attract and keep their attention.

I had also inherited a group called Sing 'n Sign, for which I served as faculty advisor. It consisted largely of students or former students from sign language classes. The group performed in sign language and song simultaneously. At practice sessions, I took words and gave them signs. They took the signs and gave me a musical event. I was the one who came out ahead. Sing 'n Sign brought back the memory of sound, something I had been in danger of losing.

My recollection of what music was like had been fading as I grew older. For years, I had used music as a cure for insomnia. When I couldn't sleep, I'd build a symphony in my head, the way other people counted sheep. I'd start with the string section of my imaginary orchestra and get the instruments playing the way I thought they should sound, then move to another section. If I had the entire orchestra going but was still awake, I'd throw in a soloist and dream up a voice or start building a ballet onstage.

I could no longer dream up symphonies, and I was desperate for some way to hold onto my memories of music. My imaginary sound had once packed as much emotional power as the real thing. Sing 'n Sign members and my students filled the breach beautifully. Many of them were gifted musicians. They had wildly eclectic tastes, including Barry Manilow, Amy Grant, Tina Turner, and Dan Fogelburg.

Because some of my students were music therapy majors, they often asked me to test their theories about music and deafness. They were curious about what I could hear. Their questions forced me to search for ways to describe my world, in which I could hear everything but nothing. The sound I actually heard with my hearing aid had little character, but what my imagination and memory could add was significant.

After a couple of years, I encouraged them to keep diaries in which they could share their thoughts or ask me questions. It was a good way to have a private, ongoing discussion with them. Some were very open in their journals because they didn't have to risk public ridicule when they wrote to me. My responses explained such things as how it was possible to drive a car without hearing, how I used interpreters at meetings, and how I communicated with Fred.

With my students, I discovered things that captured or carried sound vibrations. We learned that balloons were great, and so were milk cartons.

Two former students even looked for a way to include me in their joint recital. They defied convention by seating me on the stage near the piano they would be playing. It was an odd feeling to be looking at the audience instead of being in it, but what a grand gesture it was!

I was an unorthodox teacher; I liked to keep my students off balance and wondering what I'd do next. It gave them an added incentive to come to class. I had read that being a teacher required a high degree of showmanship, and I believed it.

Rather than requiring rote memorization of a list of signs, I decided to use the language of music that my students loved best. I searched for songs and poems around which I could build lesson plans. My students practiced more when they had something that was fun to practice with. They laughed with me as they learned signs to Shel Silverstein's poems or "The Purple People Eater."

My years as a teacher were very beneficial. After working with a lot of beginning signers, I knew the most common mistakes they made and could understand even the most pathetic signs. I also had a chance to test theories. There seemed to be a correlation between musical talent and skill at signing, and the instinct for rhythm was also an asset.

Handshape, where the hand is placed, and what movement is involved are three important elements of signing, along with the crucial facial expression, and body language. My Two-out-of-three Theory for beginners came from watching many people with the correct handshape and movement grope to remember where it should be placed. I teased my students by telling them that they would finally be real signers when they could remember all the elements and they had a dream in which they used sign language.

I took my teaching seriously and felt it was important to keep improving my skills. At Shenandoah College, I taught Pidgin Sign English, which was the sign method I used in my daily life. With Pidgin Sign English, or PSE, I signed as I spoke, using English word order but often borrowing from the signs of American Sign Language. I had many friends who used American Sign Language (ASL) and I wanted to become more fluent in it, so I signed up for a summer class in ASL at Gallaudet University. Angie Papke came with me to study interpreting, and we shared a dorm room on campus.

At one time, like so many other people who had not tried to learn American Sign Language, I thought it was used only by people too lazy or stupid to master signing in English word order. I had found ASL confining. Using PSE I could make the sign for *beautiful, gorgeous, striking,* or *pretty* while mouthing the word to make my choice clear. This appealed to my writer's heart, in love with the nuances of the English language.

I didn't realize that skilled ASL signers could show similar nuances with facial expression and body movement that changed the meaning as surely as an English word did. The more I devoted myself to studying ASL, the more I began to appreciate its richness. The arch of an eyebrow, the expansiveness of a movement, or a slight change in posture all added interesting meanings to a sign. The masters of ASL wrote as skillfully with their bodies as any of the best authors I had read.

I had gone to the Gallaudet campus for a few brief visits since my Spring Week trip in college, but it had little to offer me when I wasn't a skilled signer. This time was different. I never knew that going to school could be such a pleasure. I had always gone to classes in places that were geared for hearing people. And I had always been an exception. At Gallaudet, being deaf was ordinary and acceptable. I had never experienced such liberation.

When I went to the cafeteria, I could ask questions about the food and easily understand the answers. If I stopped at the student center to ask for information or grabbed someone on the recreation staff to ask the hours for the weight room, I had no worries. Everyone knew sign language or could easily follow my "deaf voice." If they didn't, it was judged to be some fault of theirs, not mine.

There were no raised eyebrows at my high-pitched voice and no fumbles for a pen or paper. I didn't have to contend with poor lighting or people who mumbled. Everything was designed to accommodate someone like me.

My teacher signed, and so did all the other students in my class. For the first time I participated in classroom discussions. I went to lectures. I went to cultural events. Everything was new and exciting and I just could not get enough of it.

At the end of my first week at Gallaudet, I drove back to Winchester for the weekend. I needed to stock up on groceries, so I stopped at a supermarket. I walked inside the store, as I had twice a week for the past year, and suddenly, for the first time, I felt frightened. The din was unbelievable. And everywhere I looked I was surrounded by people saying things I couldn't understand. It was such a complete change from the past week that I could barely handle it. This was the world I'd grown up in, but suddenly I felt like a foreigner coming to it for the first time. I was so shocked by the depth of my feeling that I clung to my cart for several minutes before my hands stopped shaking.

I was terribly afraid because I knew that, once again, something profound had happened to me. It was a cataclysmic experience to rival the Williamsburg conference. I knew I would never be satisfied to go back to the way I had lived before. And I was afraid that the change would be one too many for Fred.

As it turned out, I found the words to explain what I was feeling, and Fred had the willingness to listen and the courage to keep adapting. Up to this point in our lives together, Fred and I had developed complex systems to make sure my deafness would cause only a minimal disruption on the lives of people around us. I wanted to dump those systems.

Elizabeth Kübler-Ross elaborated on the stages that dying patients go through in her books about death and dying. The stages were denial, anger, an attempt to bargain for more time, depression, and acceptance. They are also the stages that persons with disabilities go through when learning to cope, or choosing not to.

I was still having trouble getting out of the first stage. I was determined to be more open about my needs. I told Fred that I was no longer going to pussyfoot around my family out of fear that signing would make them uncomfortable. I was an adult. It was time to make my own choices.

I wanted to apply the same rule to our relationship with friends. If we were in a situation where I couldn't follow what was going on, I wanted to feel free to leave. I didn't want to have to carry guilt that I'd embarrassed Fred or make him feel he ought to leave because I wasn't enjoying myself.

22

It was amazing how much my short stay at Gallaudet had changed me. I had always thought that my education was a good one. I began to realize how much of my success had been in spite of, not because of, my experiences in the classroom. I hadn't known what I was missing because I'd never had anything to compare it with.

After I'd experienced my first class discussions at Gallaudet, I was bitter. I thought about the many times I'd been cheated in the past. Learning from people offered a richness that textbooks couldn't match. I was angry with myself for the many times I'd hidden my deafness. I had cut myself off from people who might have been willing to help me.

I looked at the Winchester community in which I'd lived for the past eight years, and I was like the man who saw his glass half empty instead of half full. I felt that I was surrounded by opportunities I couldn't take advantage of.

I wanted to take a class and learn to make stained glass. I wanted to go to the library and take part in the Booked for Lunch series. I wanted to drop in on a city council meeting if I felt like it. But there weren't enough skilled interpreters in my area to make those things possible, even if I'd suddenly become independently wealthy. I felt stifled.

Things were not all bleak. My sister had signed up for a class in sign language, and she was uninhibited in using her signs with me. Gayle was learning Signing Exact English, the same sign system I'd started with. It might be good for teaching English grammar, but it was terribly ponderous for a free-wheeling conversation. Still, it was a great step forward.

I had become a reformed running addict after struggling with a series of overuse-related injuries. I ran every other day and kept the distances reasonable. Fred accompanied me, and we each took charge of two dogs, using tandem leashes to keep them from wandering off. On the days when Fred was away, I'd take all four Shelties for a run. For the first mile, as my four canines surged ahead, I felt like Ben Hur in the chariot race.

I kept seeing a sleek, tanned woman run by our house on Washington Street. I was deeply envious of her energy, which managed to make my own stamina look puny. When I finally caught a glimpse of the wonder woman's face, I realized that the runner was Kathy Smart. I'd known Kathy when she lived outside of Winchester and regularly brought her kids to the library. Now she and I were living on the same street.

Kathy got me involved with a group of women runners who met once a week to run together. To be honest, the lure of running with a group was secondary to the food we porked out on after the runs. We could eat without guilt because we'd already burned off the calories we were taking in.

The members of the group took turns hosting the dinners and setting up courses for the runs. We had wide-ranging interests, which made for stimulating conversation. Kathy and several others were very easy to speechread, at least when we were sitting in small groups. Trying to speechread them while running was another story entirely. It was rare to find a person who could match me stride for stride, and speechreading people who were bouncing up and down was never easy.

Kathy and her husband, Nick, had bought an old building,

where they opened a health club. It was just five blocks down the street from my house. I became Member Number Two through a Christmas gift from Fred and soon was lifting weights every other day. Between weight training and running, I was feeling physically better than I had during most of my adult life. But my mental state still needed work.

Besides the burden of the anger I was carrying, I'd left the presidency of Handicaps Unlimited of Virginia because I couldn't ease its growing pains or be ethically comfortable with the direction in which it was headed. It had been an exquisitely painful resignation because "surrender" was a word that had never before been in my vocabulary.

I had found a new project to throw myself into. I was frustrated by the needs that couldn't be met by our Handicaps Unlimited chapter. Fred and I were regularly getting calls from people who had the same problems—lack of housing, no transportation, and school programs that weren't doing enough. That was just for starters.

Angie Papke and I fantasized on our trips about opening an independent living center in Winchester. I often griped because our state set up innovative programs mainly in metropolitan areas. Rural areas like Winchester were the last to receive services.

As luck would have it, my friends Bill Fuller and Bob Stieg of Grafton School were "can do" people with the same idea. Grafton, a residential school for children with autism and learning disabilities, was located in nearby Berryville. After some discussion, the school applied for a state grant to assist in getting our independent living project off the ground. I did the needs assessment for the grant and then watched as the wheels turned and the Shenandoah Valley Independent Living Center was born.

Meanwhile, I was being pursued by a delegation of Jehovah's Witnesses. They knew how to push my buttons. They brought their kids when they stopped by my house, and I

didn't want to make them lose face in front of the children. I
bought one of their magazines and chatted politely with them
the first time they came by. The next thing I knew, they were
regular visitors. My good friend, the incomparable Tootie, who
had recently become Mrs. Dudley Rinker, told me about a great
line she'd heard. When missionaries looking for recruits came
to the door of a woman she knew and asked "have you found
Jesus?" the woman answered, feigning shock, "No . . . have
you lost him?"

I was also getting calls and letters from wonderful people
in the area's many churches. "We're having a speaker who
signs," they'd tell me, or "We'll be signing a hymn this Sunday—will you come?"

The gestures were heartwarming, but they were still only
gestures. As much as I appreciated them, I didn't go to the
services. I dutifully told other deaf people about the events, but
they weren't enthused about attending either. Sitting through
an entire service in which we could only appreciate one hymn
or sermon was not high on our list of fun events.

I always felt rude when I didn't go. I didn't like the feeling
I should be thankful for crumbs when it was a loaf I wanted.
There were churches in other areas where interpreters con-
veyed the richness of a service from start to finish. They signed
the prayers, the scriptures, the hymns, the creeds, and the lessons. But even these churches couldn't give me the one thing I
craved most. I wanted to be able to communicate directly with
an entire congregation and enjoy the feeling of belonging to a
true religious community.

Fred was becoming increasingly restless and unhappy. At
the root of his problems was a job that no longer challenged
him. After ten years with his company, he had a lot invested
and the thought of leaving it behind was tough to face. But I
felt that a job requiring eight or more hours a day should be
spent on something that was enjoyable and, to borrow from the

sports world, the bottom line was "no pain, no gain." I was relieved when Fred made the leap and decided to leave Pfizer.

Jim Stutzman was still my only major public relations client. Working with him always gave me an opportunity to learn new things. He was a great philanthropist, and I ended up being involved in all his causes. When I worked in his office at the Chevrolet-Cadillac dealership, I didn't just focus on the car ads or his advice column. Jim asked for just as much help for the nonprofit organizations he supported, or the extremely active Rotary Club of which he was an officer. I loved working with a man who put his heart into everything he did and didn't let himself become defined only by his business.

I was worried about our loss of income while Fred looked for a new job. A call from the Virginia Department for the Deaf and Hard of Hearing was perfectly timed. An employee at the agency asked if I would be interested in doing part-time work for the new regional outreach program they were setting up. I sent my application immediately. In January 1987, I was hired to cover the Northern Virginia region.

The job seemed ridiculously simple. For the most part, I was being asked to do what I had always done. The biggest change was that I would be paid for it. I thought it would be interesting to concentrate only on working with persons who had hearing loss and attempt to cover one disability well. I would have to do a lot of traveling, but I looked forward to learning what was happening in other areas.

For some reason, Fred had always wanted a parrot. When his parents retired and moved to Florida, he spied an opportunity. There were lots of breeders in Florida. I'd had to care for twenty fish tanks in Rhode Island, and I was the adopted mother of four dogs, so I wasn't confident of my ability to dissuade him.

We flew to Florida to see Mom and Dad Heppner. While we were there, Fred dragged me to breeders and pet shops in search of the perfect bird. The choice came down to a white cockatoo or a brilliant green mealy Amazon. I was definitely not keen on the cockatoo, which kept its hungry eyes on my fingers throughout our visit. A few weeks later, when Mom and Dad Heppner drove up to visit during the Apple Blossom Festival, they brought our new kid, the Amazon. His name was Hudson Leroy Hookbill, Leroy for short.

Leroy was an amazing bird. The first week we had him, he was sweet and complacent. The second week he was a holy terror. The third week I stood my ground, and we glared eyeball to eyeball at each other. The fourth week he decided that I just might be his equal, and we became great buddies.

Leroy loved to imitate the fire trucks and ambulances going by our house or make odd noises to see how I'd react. And he was passionately fond of Barbra Streisand tapes. Male singers, with the exception of Pavarotti, rarely interested him. "Jingle Bells" on Barbra's Christmas album was his favorite selection, and we humored him by playing it year-round, much to the bewilderment of our visitors.

I was slowly becoming more comfortable with the bulldog side of myself. When I saw something that wasn't fair, I was stubborn and unyielding in my opposition to it. I followed the adage "in matters of principle, stand like a rock; in matters of taste, swim with the current." It was amazing how many people couldn't tell the difference between principle and taste.

Sharon Mistler, Linda Field Miller, and Justine Maloney were three women in the disability rights movement who made me realize that a bulldog wasn't such a bad thing to be. When they criticized injustice and stood bedrock firm, I knew it was because they cared about people. I would be proud to be identified with them.

I felt even better after I read a speech given by Senator Lowell Weicker called "Be a Flake." He had given it as a commencement address at Brunswick School in Greenwich, Connecticut in 1979. During the speech, Weicker gave examples of eight people everyone thought were "flakes, loners, kooks, or mavericks" but who succeeded in writing wrongs and changing the course of history. Weicker cited Elsie Hill, who he said, did not let a month go by without contacting him and every other officeholder to advocate women's rights. "Eventually," he confessed, "most of us had our wives or secretaries listen to the rantings of this 'lunatic' once we were told it was Miss Hill on the phone." He recalled that Hill died one week before the U.S. House of Representatives passed the Equal Rights Amendment in 1970, and he recognized her influence on its passage with the simple statement "Elsie Hill, what magnificent lunacy."

Weicker closed his remarks by saying,

> *I'm not advocating mass protests or a revolution. Those happenings involve thousands, thus enjoying a popularity which immediately draws into question the propriety of the cause.*
>
> *No. Be a flake, a loner, a kook, a maverick on behalf of somebody or something.*
>
> *These are great concepts of the Bill of Rights that need advocacy.*
>
> *There are people out there more than you can imagine who are hurt, who are poor, who are starving, who are without hope—and who have been very much left alone. So bring one home—not to your parent's house but to your heart.*
>
> *To do that and especially to do it alone will make you the envy of the world.*

23

I thought my new job working for the Department for the Deaf and Hard of Hearing would be interesting and challenging. It definitely was. What I didn't predict was that it would be painful.

Now that I talked daily with other people who were trying to cope with hearing loss, I saw clear patterns to tough problems. I felt keenly the frustrations of the people I'd been hired to serve. There wasn't much they were going through that I hadn't already wrestled with. I cared about them deeply and could not stop worrying about their problems. Everything hit too close to home.

As I became more acquainted with the Deaf community, I was saddened to discover that it sometimes copied the less admirable things about the hearing world. The Miss Deaf America pageant was an example. It was incongruous to me that the Deaf community supported this pageant that rewarded young deaf women for their physical attractiveness. The Deaf community was still being persecuted for using sign language, facial expressions, and body movements that looked strange to ignorant and insensitive people. Somehow I expected more from them; I thought they should be fighting the stereotype associated with the notion that the way people looked was most important.

I listened to their arguments about how the competitions were more than beauty contests. My friends told me that the Miss Deaf America contest helped build character and poise. They said that the cash prizes were beneficial because they were used toward the contestants' educations. These friends of mine claimed that the contests were based on talent and good personality as well as looks.

The arguments didn't win me over. There were too many other ways to build character and poise. A trip to the Appalachians to see how people with no income survived each day with grace seemed a better choice. I couldn't help wondering how much more money there would be for scholarships if the women weren't spending it to buy gowns and pay travel expenses to attend the pageants. And no one could tell me about the last time the judges chose an overweight Miss Deaf America who blew them away with her talent and intelligence.

People who experienced hearing loss had to contend with an educational system that often didn't give them much of a shot at qualifying for good jobs. Positive role models surfaced only occasionally, and small bits of hope could be routinely taken away. In the United States, deaf and hard of hearing citizens could easily become strangers in their own land.

With all the stress, there were few professionals in the mental health system who clearly understood what hearing loss did to people. I saw marriages breaking up, people with addictive personalities, and garden-variety messed-up psyches. The calls I received from people who needed counseling and treatment programs were utterly depressing. I didn't feel confident sending them to most mental health counselors. The few professionals I knew who understood the needs of deaf or hard of hearing clients had more work than they could handle, and thus had a tendency to burn out quickly. There weren't cracks in the mental health system so much as there were gaping holes.

I kept looking for purple polka-dotted hearing aids as I traveled across my territory. Hearing aids were selling more briskly than they had in the past because they were becoming small and powerful enough to fit totally inside the ear. People seemed to think that the in-the-ear hearing aids were invisible and thus much more acceptable. They weren't as concerned as I thought they should be about controls that were so small they could barely adjust them.

I was hoping to see a change in attitude. For years we heard the phrase "men seldom make passes at girls who wear glasses." Then eyeglasses became a fashion accessory and designers put their names on frames. I was disappointed to see that the hearing aid industry hadn't copied the trend. I was sick of pink and brown flesh-colored hearing aids, a real insult to hearing aid wearers, most of whom don't have skin of that horrid tint.

I was concerned about the many people who downplayed how little they could hear. I knew firsthand how destructive that could be. Some tried to back poor hearing with sophisticated hearing aids and listening systems but failed miserably. It was hard for me to keep from preaching about the wonders of sign language and how much it had changed my life. But I knew that others had to be ready and willing to change and that it was a choice that no one else could make for them.

On the opposite end of the spectrum, I met people who had more hearing than I did and refused to wear hearing aids, use listening systems, or try to improve their skills in speech and speechreading. It seemed a curious waste of potential. At the same time, I recognized that many of them had adjusted much better to hearing loss than I had. They didn't seem at all concerned by what they might be missing.

Having worked with people who had given birth to the

national and state independent living movements served me in good stead. I had learned the hard way to embrace their principles. Back when I was working with the Telephone Pioneers to distribute teletypewriters, I enjoyed helping deaf people by making all kinds of arrangements for them. They had started coming to me whenever anything went wrong. If their teletypewriters jammed or ran out of printer paper, they showed up on my doorstep. It finally dawned on me that I had helped them get those teletypewriters so that they could become more independent, but they had just exchanged one dependency for another. I was as guilty of breeding the dependency as hearing people had been. I discovered that it was much more rewarding for all of us if I taught people to fish instead of feeding them.

I had a lot of problems finding qualified sign language interpreters. There were no certified interpreters in Winchester, and the closest lived about an hour away. As I traveled closer to the metropolitian area of Northern Virginia, I found interpreters were more abundant, but then, so were deaf people. A few individuals had the potential to become good interpreters, and they were better than nothing in a pinch. Angie could interpret meetings for me when she could hear well, but many rooms had acoustics that left her totally defeated.

The interpreting profession had its share of con artists. I found people who highly overrated their talents after completing classes in sign language or interpreting. They hadn't learned enough to be frightened by the situations in which they were called to interpret. Unfortunately, people who had never studied signs or associated with deaf people didn't know how to judge an interpreter's skills. They also didn't know about certification and screening programs. The con artists fed on their ignorance.

Sometimes deaf people themselves unwittingly helped the scam by saying nothing. When faced with the choice between help from a person who interpreted badly and no help at all, the choice was easy to make. I was as guilty as anyone else of bending to that pressure. If twelve people were attending a meeting, I felt that I could not ask them all to reschedule and come back again because my interpreter was a loser.

Working with older deaf persons gave me many of my most depressing experiences. The phrase "dying of loneliness" took on new meaning when I visited nursing homes. Some of the deaf residents had worked and raised families while sheltered by the warmth of their friends in the Deaf community, only to be sent to these homes when their families could no longer provide the constant, skilled care they needed. Others were latecomers to deafness, experiencing drastic hearing loss with age.

I found them surrounded by staff and other residents who could not communicate with them. Many of the deaf residents had retreated from life so totally that it was hard to tell if they had become mentally ill or were suffering from a degenerative disorder. I looked into the eyes of some of these older deaf people and saw nothing. I wondered if they had fantasy worlds to sustain them like those I had once created. When I talked with some of the nursing home residents who knew sign language, I could see the edges blur between what was real and what was not. They told me stories of things that never happened, mixed with events that did.

My heart would break a little each time I visited nursing homes. At one home, a woman of about eighty years of age would lie in her room for days and even weeks, almost in a state of hibernation. She depended totally on sign language to communicate. I was the only sign language user who ever visited her, so I was her only contact with the world. When I arrived, she was like a person possessed. Suddenly, she wanted to tell me everything, go everywhere.

I never learned to deal with the rage and frustration I felt on those visits. I found myself worrying incessantly about what happened when I was not there. There were a few nursing and retirement homes where deaf people could be among equals, but they were located far from the area I served.

I also hated visiting sheltered workshops. In many of them there were deaf adults whom time had passed by. They didn't necessarily have other disabilities; they simply had grown up with little schooling or had been failed by the schools they attended. Some were raised by families in which "deaf" equaled "defective," and they were kept at home and hidden from the neighbors.

Because the deaf participants in workshops were few and far between, they were very isolated. The staff rarely had skills to work effectively with them, and there were few other deaf people with whom they could try to establish friendships.

24

I had to wrestle with my negative feelings about people with hearing loss who took handouts such as government disability payments. I felt that these handouts diminished the person who accepted them. They perpetuated the misconception that deaf and hard of hearing people could not work or have rewarding lives without the charity of others. I agreed with Si Kahn, who wrote the lyric, "Whatever things are given to us will always be theirs, not ours."

But I understood reality. It was difficult to find jobs with good wages, and employer attitudes were not changing fast. People who were deaf or hard of hearing needed some source of income to survive. I knew I was fortunate to have a hearing husband who could find work easily and provide me with a second income to live on. I was in no position to judge others.

I had similar feelings about special treatment such as reduced ticket prices for theater events or lower transportation fares for persons with disabilities. The subsidies did make it possible for some people to stretch a meager paycheck. But I rarely took advantage of them because doing so robbed me of hard-won self-esteem.

I read British author Lorraine Fletcher's book, *Bens' Story*. It was a wonderful recounting of the struggle she and her husband had as they tried to do the right thing for their deaf child. One passage in the book did trouble me. Fletcher mentioned that she wanted her deaf son, Ben, to have a chance to be equal to hearing children. Yet she wrote about her joy when, one day, Ben received a number for things for free. Wherever she took him, hearing people who discovered Ben's deafness became magnanimous. Ben got free pony rides, free candy, and his mother thought it was wonderful. It must have been a delight for her to see things come to Ben without a fight, since she'd seen him through so many of those. But that somewhat insignificant passage in the book struck a jarring note with me. It brought me pell-mell back to my unanswered question—must the choice always be between respect and reward?

I hated the way Fred was penalized because he chose to marry a deaf woman. Had he married someone with good hearing, he wouldn't have faced the financial burden of hearing aids, batteries, speech therapy, caption decoders, and telecommunication devices. We'd have had money for lots of other things without these expenses. There were also other costs that were difficult to tally, like the extra driving I had to do because I couldn't reach people by telephone, or the jump in our electric bill when I couldn't hear that I'd left appliances running.

My mixed feelings about handouts emerged during a Quota Club project with Shenandoah College's Summer Music Theatre. A grant from the Virginia Commission for the Arts funded a special performance of one of the theatre's popular offerings. Quota Club agreed to pay for two top-flight sign language interpreters.

The special performance was designed to give persons with disabilities a chance to see a show, free of charge. This was the first time many of them were able to experience a theater performance. The event also marked the first time that any performance of any theater in the area had used sign language interpreters. I was among those in the audience, so I saw firsthand how much the deaf attendees appreciated this opportunity to participate.

The response to that first special performance was so positive that it became an annual event. But, sadly, these performances were just another glorified handout. They were held on a weekday afternoon, at the beginning of the show's run. The performances were more of a final dress rehearsal than a polished product. This gave the impression that the audience wasn't sophisticated or worthy enough for a more professional show.

Only a few deaf people saw the musicals because they were held during working hours. The college didn't try to integrate interpreters with its regular performances. This gave deaf individuals no choice of which of the several musicals they'd like to attend, or when. The choices were all made for them.

Because many deaf people lacked experience in standing up for themselves, they were at a disadvantage. They frequently shared their deepest feelings with me, but they were reluctant to talk to the people who needed to hear their concerns. All too often, I was still called upon to play the "bad guy."

Helping deaf and hard of hearing people to build their self-confidence was often a slow process. But I figured that somebody had to make a start and it might as well be me. I had tremendous confidence in the people who came to me for help. They were great untapped resources, and I couldn't wait for the rest of the world to realize it.

Old habits were hard to break. Many persons with hearing loss became so cut off from life that they lost confidence in their ability to deal with people. A lot of them felt they were being a bother when they asked for something that required a little extra effort from someone. It was amazing to me that we made such poor advocates for ourselves.

I met many people who were eager to help improve services where they worked. They took sign language classes and helped me get TDDs placed in their offices. I trained them to recognize and respond to calls. Some began to actively look for opportunities to hire persons who had a hearing loss. Training them was great fun.

Unfortunately, these highly motivated people were appreciated by their bosses as well as by me. They were always being transferred or promoted. Nevertheless, they often became so frustrated that they quit their jobs. Turnover was my great enemy, because these folks were usually replaced by far less motivated people who had no commitment to the cause.

The word "commitment" was the key. I found a frustrating pattern, no matter whether I was working with a hospital, police department, library, bank, or drug store. If there wasn't at least one person in the place who was committed to improving services to deaf and hard of hearing persons, and who had the clout to make sure other people did the same, my best efforts would fail. I could place TDDs, provide interpreter referral lists, and train people until I was blue in the face, but nothing would really change.

I saw a lot of the "dust cover syndrome," a common disease that affected offices. I'd set up a TDD, train the staff, and then tell deaf and hard of hearing people about the office's new services. Sooner or later I'd get callers who complained that they'd tried unsuccessfully to get through to a new TDD I'd told them about. When I followed up on the complaint, I found that the staff hadn't responded to the call because, basically, they lacked commitment. They used a lot of excuses—"too busy to answer," "forgot how to use the TDD," "the person you trained was out to lunch." The one excuse that made me most crazy (and I heard it many times) was that they didn't remember how to remove the hard plastic dust cover from their TDD.

Sometimes other professionals in the field of human services were much more discouraging than those individuals afflicted with the dust cover syndrome. I met one woman who complained at length about the state schools for the deaf. She thought they were terrible schools because they were turning out graduates who couldn't read or write well and had few skills.

This woman had spent some years making a living trying to find jobs for deaf students. She claimed that the deaf students who took classes with hearing students in mainstreamed schools were much easier to work with.

I thought she was being far too quick to sling mud. Blaming the shortcomings in reading and writing skills of its graduates on the schools for the deaf was pretty simplistic. There was plenty of blame to go around.

The "successful" kids produced by mainstreamed schools often turned out to have important advantages over kids in deaf-only schools. Some were like me; they became deaf after they had a language base, so English was their native language. Learning to read it and write it wasn't that much of a stretch. Some had hearing losses that were far less severe than those of the kids who were attending schools for the deaf. And some just happened to be fortunate kids who were born with a gift for language.

I also knew that students who attended mainstreamed schools had a better chance of having involved parents. Many of the best students I'd met had parents who encouraged their natural curiosity and creativity. That was hard for parents to do with a child who came home only on weekends.

Superior reading and writing skills aside, I wondered just how well-adjusted those mainstreamed kids were. Some of them had little or no contact with peers or adults who had hearing loss.

Schools for the deaf were also being viewed as if they were as second-class as the kids who went to them. They didn't get the funding they needed for good staff support and purchase of materials. And they constantly fought against becoming dumping grounds. Children who were failed by mainstreamed schools, when they finally arrived at schools for the deaf, carried all kinds of emotional baggage from the mainstreaming experience. No magic formula could wipe out years of neglect and misguided approaches.

On the other hand, I knew that some schools for the deaf were guilty of expecting too little from their students or still insisted on teaching the child in a language he or she could not understand. There was plenty of room for improvement in all quarters.

That professional's harsh words about schools for the deaf struck me as being most unfair because she had very poor skills in American Sign Language. If she had been able to communicate better in the language these graduates used, she might have discovered skills, talents, and interests galore.

It came as no surprise that she didn't look forward to working with them, because everything from filling out forms to on-the-job training demanded more work on her part. It was certainly easier to place the less-deafened clients who had the best English skills. There was no incentive to work with people who required more help when her job performance was being judged by the number of placements.

I wondered about the whole argument over the low reading scores of the average deaf high school graduate, which hovered steadily at the level of illiteracy. The graduates' poor performance was often blamed on the poor quality of education in schools for the deaf. With so many other factors involved, that blame smacked of buck passing if not criminal negligence.

Nobody was blameless, since hearing kids were graduating with poor reading skills, too. I had one student in my college sign language classes who—honest to God—wrote an entire paper about the problems of "dea*th* people."

Illiteracy is troublesome in a nation peppered with public libraries that give everyone an opportunity to read, learn, and grow. But I couldn't understand why we kept allowing educators to point to the dismal reading level of deaf persons as if it were evidence of educational failure.

It seemed we weren't using good analogies. Hearing students who graduated from high school after studying a foreign language could sometimes read that language better than a deaf person could read English. But how well would that hearing kid have learned Latin or French or Spanish if he or she didn't have the reinforcement of hearing it or being able to use a native language to explain its intricacies?

Research was beginning to show clearly that the visual language of signs was the native language of persons who were born deaf or deafened when they were very young. Yet we continued to judge their educational success not by their fluency in that language but by their success in one that was foreign— English. Students who graduated with skill in English were not being recognized as the gifted linguists they were.

25

For years I had focused a lot of my attention on trying to make the local hospital more accessible to deaf patients. I worked with renewed vigor after I took my job with the state.

Years earlier, one of my projects had been to place a teletypewriter in the Winchester hospital and try to get a policy that would require the use of qualified sign language interpreters. The hospital had considered the provision of those things a charity; I thought of them as a necessity.

Tootie had arranged for the teletypewriter donation. To our dismay, the teletypewriter had been stored in a closet where no one knew about it. We retrieved it from the closet and trained the staff to use it. Then I spent the next seven years trying unsuccessfully to ensure telephone access. Deaf people needed the same things from hospitals that hearing people did—information about poison, answers to questions about their bills, or the chance to talk to family and friends who were patients. They just couldn't get these things for any number of reasons. Mostly, the problem boiled down to the same old lack of commitment and willingness to change.

From my teenage years onward, I had never been a person who simply broke bones or got cuts. I had spectacular accidents. I'd spent enough time in hospital emergency rooms to know that I didn't want to go back.

Once, after a mishap while playing volleyball, I needed stitches in my chin. I was fortunate that Fred was with me in the emergency room. A sheet of white paper was placed over my face, with a hole only at the area to be stitched. While I lay blind as well as deaf, I felt something cool and wet touch my arm.

I found out later that I'd been swabbed with alcohol. Fred heard the nurse say "this will sting a bit" and, horrified, he had stopped her just as she was about to give me a tetanus booster. She had forgotten that I could neither see nor hear. A good man, Fred. He knew it would be hard to explain how I came to have a stitch through my nose.

The medical horror stories I heard from other deaf and hard of hearing people were much more frightening. A deaf man told me about a time when his mother was very ill. A hospital staff member asked him to sign some papers. He couldn't understand what the papers were for because he'd never been a good reader. But he was under a lot of pressure and there was no sign language interpreter to help him. He understood that the papers were very important to the hospital and that the surgery his mother needed couldn't be done without his signature. So he gave it. Later he discovered that his signature not only authorized surgery but also made him responsible for the expenses related to his mother's treatment. I never forgot the anguish in his eyes when he told me about all the things his wife and children had to do without while he paid off his mother's medical bills.

Uninformed consent was a problem for other deaf people. I heard about a woman who didn't realize she'd signed papers authorizing a hysterectomy. She was devastated because she desperately wanted more children. Another woman couldn't understand the instructions when the nurse handed her a suppository. She ate it and became much more ill.

I found that such medical horror stories were common among deaf and hard of hearing people. Asking about experiences with doctors was a great ice breaker. Several people told me they'd been stuck in waiting rooms much longer than necessary because they couldn't tell when their names had been called. That had happened to me often enough that a blood pressure reading in a doctor's office was bound to be skewed. I watched so tensely for my name to be called that I was jumpy before I ever saw the doctor.

My friends with hearing loss complained about the way doctors and nurses talked to their husbands and kids instead of to them. People who became deaf later in life told me they couldn't believe how little help doctors had been in pointing them toward resources for understanding and coping with their hearing loss.

I did a survey of doctors in my region and found that not one ear, nose, and throat specialist (ENT) had a TDD in his or her office. Although these were the specialists on whom we most depended for information about our ears, we couldn't even call them without assistance. In more than thirty years as a deaf person, I had never met an ENT who knew sign language or basic fingerspelling or took an active interest in the Deaf community.

I was amused and irritated to have numerous hospital staff persons tell me that they rarely had patients who were deaf. One nurse made that statement at the exact moment when a deaf person I knew was recovering three floors above us. That was a major drawback to having a disability that is invisible. Several doctors told me that they had no trouble communicating with their deaf patients. I had a hard time believing that when I saw how badly they scrawled their prescriptions.

If I wanted to get fighting mad, nothing worked better than visiting a deaf or hard of hearing friend who was a patient in the hospital. I couldn't believe how many nurses would chatter at people whose glasses and hearing aids were sitting in plain view on the bedside table. Worse, they stood and talked in front of bright windows while my poor friends squinted at them.

It was always difficult to explain to medical professionals why it was important to use certified sign language interpreters. Many hospitals had language banks in which they listed people with sign language skills. But these signers on their lists weren't necessarily qualified to interpret. Many were volunteers who were delighted to be able to do something helpful and were unaware of how their incompetence could put a deaf person at risk. They could be great at bridging the gap until an interpreter was available, but they were no substitute for the real thing. Doctors who wouldn't dream of operating on their children or spouses were slow to grasp what was wrong with asking relatives or friends of a deaf person to interpret.

I was always lucky enough to have Fred with me on my trips to the hospital emergency room. Because I needed help fast and interpreters were not easy to come by in Winchester, he got pressed into service.

Fred was a wipeout helping with medical forms. He could recite the license plate numbers for his last seven cars but could never remember my social security number. All the same, his years with Pfizer, during which he showed trauma films to doctors, at dinners, had made him pretty blase about injuries. And he was on friendly terms with many of the physicians in town.

I was always reassured by Fred's presence when I was in the hospital. His accounts of things he overheard or the stories he improvised while I waited for treatment kept my mind off pain. I just wished that my doctors and nurses would remember that I liked to have their reassurance, too.

For irony, nothing came close to that provided by two brothers, Peter and Joseph Schmidt. They called me when they first took over a veterinary practice in Winchester. They'd worked with several deaf persons in the past and wanted to continue to do so. They told me they'd found deaf persons to be caring and responsible pet owners. The brothers didn't know sign language, but their philosophy was to do "whatever it takes to do the job well."

Immediately after I gave them sources for TDDs, they placed an order for one. In a town with hundreds of doctors and a major medical center, not one physician had a TDD, but they did. After they'd used the TDD for a few months, they and their office manager, Reba Barley, told me they thought they weren't responding to calls fast enough. To improve their efficiency, they installed a separate telephone line solely for use by TDD callers.

26

Fred and I were very attached to our house on Washington Street. We had been absorbed in its renovation for more than three years. Everywhere we looked, we could see something we'd sweated to fix. Our neighborhood was terrific; parties with our neighbors were frequent and fun. Each summer we got permission to close our street for one night and hold a huge block party.

In 1986, our work on the house was nearing completion, and we opened it to hundreds of visitors for a Christmas Tour to raise funds for Preservation of Historic Winchester. But our beautiful house ate money that wasn't in abundance in Fred's new career. We knew we could postpone some maintenance projects, but we couldn't bear to think about letting the house fall into disrepair.

Fred had taken a position with a company that sold both modular and log homes. He was excited about the potential of modular home building. After lots of discussion, we decided to sell our house and erect a modular in a new development to show some of the possibilities. We planned to order the shell and put in most of the finishing touches. The excitement of working on something new helped mitigate our unhappiness over moving from Washington Street.

We'd renovated one house and restored another, but Fred and I had never had a glimpse of the kind of hell involved in building a house from the ground up. We bought the property and erected the modular shell without much incident. But it took a long time for the promised and badly needed water and utility lines to go in, slowing progress on the house to a crawl. We bought a generator so that we could run power tools, but without water we had to bring paint brushes home for cleaning and take jugs over to wash up spills.

The house on Washington Street was under contract, and we had to move out of it before the new one was ready. Our friends Rosemary Green and Ron Heath had recently married; they became qualified for sainthood when they gave us the use of their basement room. We spent a horrendous six weeks living there with four dogs and a bird, sleeping on an air mattress and eating from a microwave oven.

Fred and I worked on the new house with every minute we could spare from our paying jobs. The road leading to it was slow to be paved because the road contractor was also waiting for the water and utility lines to be laid. When we tried to get to the house to work, we were alternately choked with dust or bogged down in mud after it rained.

All of us were miserable. The dogs were confused by the change in their habitat and had to be watched constantly. Several times they ran off and miraculously found their way back to our old home.

Work on the new house brought another great crisis in our marriage. We seemed to go through one disaster after another. Some of the plumbing had been improperly installed and entire wall sections had to be ripped out. While we were moving our possessions to the new house, a section of shelving in our walk-in closet collapsed. As luck would have it, two full cans of paint were on those shelves to get them out of the way of the carpet installers. When the shelves collapsed, the paint cans fell, burst open, and instantly destroyed much of my wardrobe.

With so many things going wrong, Fred and I started to take our frustrations out on each other. I felt as if everything in my life was out of control, and there was nothing I could do about it. There was, however, one thing I could do, and I did it expeditiously. I changed my hair color. But I found that blondes do not have more fun.

In the middle of this summer of our discontent, Toby's health began to fail. She was thirteen years old and had served as my ears with the utmost loyalty and distinction. The veterinarian told me that little could be done because her body was simply shutting down from old age. With the rest of my life in chaos, I couldn't bear the thought of losing Toby. I nursed her around the clock, and she gradually pulled out of the crisis, though she never completely regained her strength. She seemed to know that I still needed her. Months later, when peace was again restored, she had kidney failure from which she did not recover.

Three months after Toby's death, Mac, the only male in the pack, suddenly became violently ill and we lost him, too. It was a tremendous blow because he had been perfectly healthy until the day he died. His magnanimous, happy-go-lucky personality was irreplaceable.

Fred had learned about a log cabin for sale just across the state line in West Virginia. We drove out to see it. I wasn't immediately excited about the cabin; it had been built for a man who must have loved brown, a color of which I was not a fan. Everything in the cabin, from the bathroom tile to the kitchen counter, seemed to be some variation on a tree trunk. But the wooded mountains surrounding the cabin were magnificent, and I fell instantly in love with the character of the cabin's seller, who owned a lovingly restored house across the field.

The timing for the purchase was all wrong. Our new house was stretching our financial resources to the limit. I figured that the cabin would make or break our marriage, either by causing stress or by relieving it.

To my surprise, the cabin became my salvation. Fred and I tried to spend at least two weekends a month there. It was the one place in which we could truly relax. The summer rains brought a profusion of wildflowers to the fields, attracting butterflies, bees, and hummingbirds. The woods were pungent with the smell of pine, bringing memories of the forests I'd loved in Maine and Pennsylvania. As I hiked through the woods, I once again felt the peace that had sustained me as a child. It was as if the trees drew me in and spoke softly to me through the gentle breezes that stirred their branches. Our cabin had no telephone, so there was nothing from our "other life" to intrude on the peace.

Over the years I had forgotten how to be still. I was so used to working frenetically and juggling numerous projects that I had never slowed down long enough to totally absorb the lessons I'd been learning. My weekends in West Virginia had a way of reminding me of what was really important. It became harder and harder to keep going back to the pressures of life in Winchester.

Gradually I realized that those pressures were of my own making. My work with other people who had lost their hearing remained enormously stressful because it brought me face to face with myself everyday. When they talked about their feelings of alienation from their families and friends, the discrimination they faced in jobs and education, or their frustration at not being able to use a telephone, I understood perfectly. They told me how they felt clumsy when they learned their first signs. And they were tired of reminding people that they needed to see lips or explaining to them how hard it was to hear over background noise.

I loved the people I had chosen to serve, and I loved the satisfaction of watching them become empowered. But I had made their pain mine and it was tearing me up.

I decided that I needed to get out of human services. I was

frustrated at how little progress I was able to make despite the long hours I was working.

I had found that no matter how many hours I put in, there was never enough time to do everything that needed to be done. I had tried unsuccessfully for years to be a person who could stop caring at the end of the day. I thought that if I got back into public relations again, maybe I could find a balance in my life and the pain and guilt I felt for not doing enough would go away.

I was very disappointed at the lack of opportunities in Winchester. I had lived there for more than ten years, during which the town had grown enormously. But there were still few professional jobs in fields that interested me, and not enough clients like Jim Stutzman. I was also unhappy with the slow pace of change in my adopted city. There were still only a handful of TDDs in offices, and for all the years I'd paid taxes, I'd never been able to follow a city council meeting. Interpreters at meetings and captioning of local news programs looked to be a long way off.

I had no luck finding a good public relations position even when I looked in the more progressive areas closer to the nation's capital. I found that job discrimination was still alive, but much more subtle.

Meantime, the outreach program for which I was working had been picking up support across the state, and I had a shot at becoming a full-time employee of my state agency. That would make me eligible for benefits like retirement and health insurance, which were becoming more attractive to me as each birthday passed.

The full-time hours weren't much of an incentive, since I was already putting in forty-hour weeks but not claiming all the hours. I decided to see if I could accomplish more by living in a central location. Winchester was at the far western end of my territory. I thought I might feel more like I was moving ahead if I could free up some of the time I was wasting on the road.

Fred and I chose to move to Reston, the central point in my territory. We liked the seriousness with which the community protected its trees and the fifty miles of paved and lighted paths, perfect for running and bicycle riding. We had finished building our enormous modular home and found a buyer for it. It was a wrench to leave our many friends in Winchester and my wonderful traveling companion, Angie. But I was ready to make the jump for reasons that went well beyond my job.

I wanted to do something I had never done before: start off in a new place with a clean slate and try to live as an honest person. In Reston, I vowed to be open about my deafness and my needs from the beginning.

27

Fred and I found a tiny ground-floor apartment that allowed pets. We'd decided to rent for a while, even though we were living in cramped quarters, because we wanted to get to know the Reston area before we invested in another home.

We'd lived in the modular house for several months while we completed work on it. Once again we were caught between houses, closing on the modular two weeks before our apartment was ready. Fortunately, this time we had the cabin to fall back on. We moved everything we could out there and commuted to our jobs for a few hectic days.

I had several bad nights during the seven months we lived in the Reston apartment. Our bedroom faced a parking lot, and there were a number of residents who kept a vigorous night life. Strong beams from the headlights on cars returning late at night or leaving early in the morning kept penetrating our venetian blinds. The flood of light would register on my slumbering brain, and I'd wake up, adrenalin pumping madly, expecting to confront a roaring fire.

I had always had a problem with my sensitivity to light. I knew lots of kids who were afraid of the dark. Unlike those kids, I was unable to sleep with a light on. If someone forgot to turn the light off in the hallway, I'd wake up and be unable to sleep again until I'd flipped the switch. When I traveled, it had become a ritual to block every light source before settling for the night. The lighted display on a videocassette recorder or luminous numbers on an alarm clock were enough to keep me tossing restlessly.

Our tolerance for the apartment ran out quickly. Fred and I were falling over each other and the dogs from the first day. I used a corner of the tiny kitchen for my office, and Fred put his desk in the bedroom. For the first time in fifteen years, we had to share a bathroom, and we quickly remembered why we stopped doing so in the first place.

Fred had switched careers again. He'd obtained his real estate license but opted to start working as a home inspector. It was a great match for the skills he'd developed over the years and ideal for someone who hated paperwork but loved to be with people. One of the added attractions was in meeting other home inspectors. The profession seemed to attract lots of eccentrics. Fred was meeting people from a wide range of backgrounds from architecture to construction, but all tended to be mavericks with wide-ranging intelligence.

Through his contacts in the real estate business, Fred found a townhouse about a mile from our apartment. We were happy to stretch out again, get our furniture out of storage, and let the dogs out into a fenced backyard. The townhouse also had three bathrooms, with room for a fourth.

I had moved so many times during the past five years that I was becoming conscious of how much adaptation my deafness required in new surroundings. I had a vintner's nose, despite the fact that it had been broken and battered many times since I was thirteen. I noticed new and unusual smells, and my brain was ready to switch to red alert whenever my nose recognized something burning.

Once, when Fred and I were on vacation in San Francisco, I had smelled smoke while watching television in our hotel room. The two of us checked up and down the hall but saw nothing amiss. Still, I was certain I smelled something burning. I insisted that Fred call the front desk to report the odor. The concierge thanked us politely for the call and told us that the restaurant's cook had accidentally charred one of his creations. He lied, but my nose didn't. The next morning's newspaper reported that a fire had broken out in a storage room several floors below.

When a teakettle or a pot came to a boil, I could tell by sensing the vibrations if I touched the handle. I felt the water as it bubbled and rolled. My sense of touch was often the one requiring the most attention in my new house. I was perplexed for several weeks by a sort of 'ka-thud, ka-thud' rhythm I felt only when I was in the kitchen. Through process of elimination, I discovered that Leila sent this tactile warning whenever she walked into the room. Her curious gait, which developed after an accident, could be picked up easily because the kitchen had no padding between the plywood floor and the carpet.

In fact, the kitchen floor became a chatty friend. It lurched a bit when the washing machine was running, hummed when the dishwasher was on, and really got rhythm when the dryer was at work.

I learned to tell when the wild birds fed most heavily. My small friends made gentle flickers of light and cast shifting shadows on the walls when their wings slashed the sunlight as they flew to our feeders for sustenance. The patterns their shadows made also told me what was happening outside. A large shadow lifting in one great movement meant they had been startled to sudden flight. That gave me a cue to look outside, where I often found a postman making rounds or a repairman coming up the sidewalk.

Tam and Leila, our two remaining Shelties, were elderly. Leila took her age gracefully, but Tam reminded me of myself. She had never learned to slow down. Although she'd had a bad heart for years, she was still full of energy.

When Tam's health finally started to fail, it did so quickly. Within three months of the first hint she was losing ground, she had a massive heart attack and died in my arms.

Leila luxuriated in having our total attention during her last months. I spent as much time with her as possible; she had an incredibly sweet personality and acted unfailingly cheerful even when I was certain she must be uncomfortable. She needed a great deal of nursing, but I was happy to give it. Eventually she joined the other three dogs in the graveyard overlooking the cabin. Our house and lives seemed unbearably empty without our four-legged family. I was sorely tempted to get a puppy, but I had applied to a hearing dog program and a second dog in the house would disrupt the bonding process between me and the hearing dog, when it arrived.

Leroy wasn't complaining. He had turned into a first class watchbird. He became protective of me and suspicious of every visitor. Fred brought back some large limbs that were downed by a lightning storm at the cabin. We propped them up on heavyweight Christmas tree stands to make climbing trees for Leroy—he loved to play in their branches and rip them to shreds with his beak.

28

In July 1989, I attended the Deaf Way conference. The speakers were wonderful and the companionship was peerless. But I realized keenly that I had been raised apart from the Deaf culture on which the conference was based. There were times when I still ached to belong to something.

Shortly before the conference, Fred and I had gone to Maine to spend a week with my family. We all rented a cottage at Old Orchard Beach across from the one owned by the Woodhouses.

I'd hated the "vacation." I still had been unable to resolve the feelings caused by my family's unconscious rejection. I tried to focus on the positive and pace my visits with them carefully to avoid depression. I was doing well at keeping my emotions under control with elaborate little schemes.

I probably disliked my week at Old Orchard Beach more than necessary because I had unrealistic expectations for it. I wanted to recapture the feelings I'd had there during some of the happiest times of my life. But the great days I'd enjoyed at the beach had been ones in which I was hearing or my life was far less complicated.

My alienation from my family was becoming more pronounced because of a strange twist. Shortly before the move to

Reston, I became so frustrated by Fred's recurring migraines and chronic stomach irritation that I immersed myself in some serious library research. After boning up on diet and nutrition and testing some food combinations, we discovered that Fred was not only lactose-intolerant but also had problems digesting any kind of animal-based protein.

Eliminating meat and dairy products from our meals caused a dramatic improvement in Fred's health. I joined Fred in a vegan diet to help eliminate the temptation for him to cheat, and I immediately felt much stronger myself. My reading about diet had also made me wary of refined foods and additives, so we gradually stopped buying anything containing them.

This, understandably, did not go over well with my meat-and-potatoes family whose traditions were largely based on food. The Christmas cookies and pumpkin pies at Thanksgiving, along with the turkey, were now *verboten*. My mother had delighted in making Fred's favorite chocolate chip cookies whenever he came to visit, but unfortunately we discovered that they triggered his allergies in no time flat. Even the box lunches we'd loved at the beach no longer had their attraction.

On the heels of the dismal week at Old Orchard Beach and the thrilling but depressing week at Deaf Way, I found that there would be a delay in hiring for full-time outreach positions. Since I had been working too many hours for a part-time state employee, I was told to cut back drastically.

It was another summer of major frustration. I had moved to Reston so that I could accomplish more, not less. There was plenty of work to be done, and I wanted to bury myself in it so I could forget about my unresolved problems with my family. To make matters worse, I'd developed a good supplemental income by doing freelance writing for a publishing company. While I was in Maine, the company had filed for bankruptcy, drying up my extra income as well as making it impossible for me to collect the hundreds of dollars they owed me.

After Deaf Way, I had started to write down some of my thoughts, thinking I'd publish an article or two. It seemed a good way to blow some of the myths about hearing loss and occupy my mandatory free time.

Instead of writing articles, I found myself pouring out years upon years of anger. I hoped writing would prove to be as good a therapy now as it had been when I was younger. My articles quickly turned into a book.

I began to have glimpses of the source of my anger. There was a frightening amount of it. I worked obsessively for over a month, writing eight or more hours each day. I felt relieved to have all my anger out in the open and hoped that my cheap stab at self-therapy would be effective.

With some of the money I'd set aside from the sale of our Winchester house, Fred and I looked for a CD player. I felt terrible when he stopped buying tapes and records because they were something only he could enjoy. It didn't escape my attention that whenever he visited my brothers, he spent a lot of time listening to their music collections.

Fred rigged the cabin to give me maximum sound thrill. Since we had no close neighbors, I could turn up the volume on the stereo system when I was alone. Fred bought a sub-woofer to add the bass sounds that were easiest for me to sense. For prime enjoyment when we watched a videotape of *Amadeus*, he connected four speakers, placed me in the middle, and bounced sound off me from all directions. It was nirvana. I was seated on the floor, and the wood from the cabin logs carried the vibrations beautifully.

Over the years I had gone through periods of guilt when I felt that I was being more of a burden to Fred than a hearing wife would be. I'd inadvertently left the car running for hours in the carport. I'd almost burned out the garbage disposal when I forgot it was churning up long-dead leftovers.

One weekend, while Fred was working in Reston, I went alone to the cabin. Unaware that workmen had messed with our plumbing, I turned on the water pump. Water immediately started to gush into the house from a valve that had been left open. By the time I discovered the mess two hours later, the water was ankle deep. To get a true measure of the disaster, I had only to watch Fred's face as he walked downstairs, where I was still bailing out five hours later. He had stored many of his beloved tools on the basement floor.

Our trickiest adjustment was brought about by my desperate search for balance. When I needed things that went beyond what other wives demanded of their husbands, I tried to keep my self-respect by offering something in return. Hagglers in the Middle Eastern markets could learn a thing or two from us.

When Fred was rushed, making a telephone call for me could command a high price on the household market—usually something I hated to do, like iron a shirt. Fred had a long torso, with shirts as big as my dresses, and they were a bitch to whip around an ironing board.

I resented the people who thought that Fred was either a nut case or a saint for marrying me. I got the flip side. When I told people that my husband was hearing, they often responded with praise or condemnation. Some members of the Deaf community were hostile when they found out that I had a hearing husband. Most warmed up a bit when I told them that Fred knew sign language.

I dubbed Fred The Lazy Signer because he cheated so much on fingerspelling. He'd learned that if he started to fingerspell a word, I could usually guess it within the first letter or two, so that was sometimes all he spelled. The combination of a few signs and a few fingerspelled letters worked effectively for us. But Fred's signing and fingerspelling abilities did not improve much over the years because they didn't have to. I was the only deaf person he saw on a daily basis. When he was around other deaf people who didn't speechread well or who signed without voicing words, he felt very awkward.

Fred made my life rich through his willingness to be my ears. When he was not being monopolized by other people, he could be an amusing and entertaining commentator. At rallies, he delighted in telling me what the crowd was chanting. On trips, he'd repeat colorful remarks or conversations he found humorous. Bus and subway rides with him were fun because he'd eavesdrop and tell me what the other passengers were saying. Thankfully, captioned television freed him from the role of tube narrator, which he performed admirably for six years.

Fred's capacity for storing information about sound had always been a source of constant amazement to me. Early in our marriage, while we were walking up a street, he told me that a Harley Davidson motorcycle was headed in our direction. I watched, astounded, as one rounded the curve and came into view. "How did you know it was going to be a Harley when you couldn't even see it?" I asked him. He explained that the engine was very distinctive.

I had always assumed that engines were engines. The idea that they could make sounds so individual that an ear could discriminate between them had never occurred to me. But Fred swore this was true, and then proved it. He stood by the curve and correctly guessed the make of most vehicles before they came into view, sometimes throwing in the year of manufacture for good measure.

In return for the favor of access to this world of sound, I tried to give gifts with my vision. My deaf person's eye for detail, journalist's training, and penchant for recording the trivial made for offbeat accounts. With the voluminous amounts of reading I did, I saved Fred hours of work by researching and providing capsule summaries on any number of subjects. In essence, I became his walking, breathing, *Reader's Digest*.

One of the most interesting things we noticed over the years was that, in drawing from different sources of information, we sometimes received totally different messages. When we talked with people, Fred would listen to what they said and I would watch what they did. Later, I might mention to Fred that a person looked troubled and I was convinced something was deeply wrong. That often came as a surprise to Fred, because nothing the person had talked about gave such an indication. But it was amazing how often I was right. Body language revealed what words did not.

Fred and I had become used to straddling two worlds and we learned to laugh at the inevitable clashes in culture. He drove me to distraction with his habit of shouting "Look!" and pointing to something in the distance, then, after I'd turned, telling me what to look for. My first response to urgency on someone's face and a pointed finger was always to turn immediately in the direction of the pointed finger. Since I didn't know what I was supposed to pick out from all the things I saw when I looked in that direction—unless it was glaringly obvious—I'd look back to Fred's lips for an explanation. By the time he told me what he wanted me to look for, it was often impossible to find. He'd get mad at me for missing the event and I'd get mad at him for being so obtuse and impatient. We were a prickly pair until we got each other trained.

We were opposites to start with when it came to internal time clocks. I functioned best in the early morning, while Fred was a bear before 9:00 a.m. Learning to live with me was a huge adjustment for him. Not only did I wake early with all my cylinders in high gear, I also seemed to wake with some oddity from the far distant memory section of my brain. Buried there were all the songs and poems I had memorized over the years, including snatches from the records my parents played when I was very young. Nothing could compare to the fun of serenading my husband at 6:00 a.m., in high-pitched monotone, with all umpteen verses of the "Ballad of the Alamo."

As I grew to appreciate both the verbal wit of the hearing world and the visual wit of native ASL signers, I felt confined by both. When I was with hearing persons, I often found myself wanting to embellish a joke with signs, facial expression, and body language to make it richer. With my deaf friends, it was the reverse. I was frustrated by my inability to translate the verbal puns of the hearing world to visual terms. It was a comfort to live with someone who could appreciate both worlds.

Fred was a good man to have around when I dropped loose change or the tiny backs from my pierced earrings, at least when they landed on the floor and not the carpet. When we married, we both agreed that we wanted a family with two or three children. We talked about adopting and becoming foster parents. There just never seemed to be a right time to get started, for a variety of reasons. Eventually we sat down to make a decision on whether we would have children at all. The idea of not having offspring was radical, but for us it was the right choice and one we became comfortable with.

────────────29────────

I was officially hired as a full-time regional outreach specialist with the Virginia Department for the Deaf and Hard of Hearing in the fall of 1990. One of my closest professional contacts was Jerry Nelson, the director of the Fairfax Resource Center for the Hearing Impaired. Jerry and I were the only deaf persons working in the human services field in all of Northern Virginia, and we were among only a handful in the entire state. I depended heavily on Jerry for his insight into some of the mutual problems we faced. When he announced that he was leaving the Resource Center to accept a faculty position at Gallaudet University, I felt bereft. He had been my total peer support system.

I was tempted by the opportunity to work in an office with staff I respected after years of playing a sort of Lone Ranger without a sidekick. I applied for Jerry's position, which had a new title. Happily for me, after a five-month national search, the Center's governing board chose someone in their own back yard. I became the Resource Center's President in January 1991.

I had struggled for years with deep jealousy about Fred's close relationship with my family. He had started to spend a good deal of time with my brother Randy.

I'd never had that kind of closeness with either of my brothers. When Randy was young, I'd read stories to him. He was more patient than my classmates and appreciated the attention even when he didn't know what I was saying. Once, when he was three or four, we were sitting side by side to share the book I was reading to him. He leaned over and shouted "Cheryl!" directly into my hearing aid to get my attention. It cracked us all up that he had figured out how I got my sound.

As we grew older, Randy and I occasionally played sports and games together. I was the person he came to with his first questions about the birds and bees. At one time, when he was in college, he had written a few letters that allowed me to see the wonderful person he was becoming. But since he'd graduated from college, we'd grown more and more out of touch with each other.

Fred told me that Randy was experiencing problems similar to some I'd had in the past. He wanted to get the two of us together because he thought I could give Randy better guidance than he could.

At his urging, I wrote Randy a letter to try to entice him to come for a visit. My letter backfired when Randy completely misunderstood my intentions. I had written what I thought was humorous and cryptic enough to make him want to come and find out more. He took the letter seriously and instead of planning a visit, wrote a response that I found insulting. In fact, Randy's letter made me so angry that I fired off another letter of my own and told him so. A lot of the anger that surfaced during my writing the previous summer spilled over into that letter.

The most amazing thing was that I actually mailed it. Randy joked later that he'd had to read my letter with asbestos gloves. But he read it, reflected on it, and then wrote me a beautiful response. For the first time, a door had opened between us, and we rushed through it together.

My parents came for a brief visit. They were on their way to a vacation in Hawaii, and Fred and I had agreed to take care of their border collie, Katie, for two weeks. Since we lived only a short distance from the airport, I told them I'd get them to their connecting flight from Washington to Chicago and pick them up when they returned.

Their flight was scheduled to leave before dawn. Although Fred had to work later that day, he offered to drive us. I was grateful for his help because I hated to drive in the dark. The four of us, with luggage but minus dog, piled into the car for the trip to the airport. Under the cover of darkness, I sat in the back seat, watching the others talk and wondering exactly why I'd bothered to come.

At the airport, each of us grabbed a suitcase and headed for the terminal. We got into a long line leading to the ticket desk, where things were chaotic. I could tell by watching the faces around me that there was some sort of problem, but I didn't know what. Mom and Dad were busy listening and talking to each other, and it was clear some kind of important decision was being made. They were involving Fred in the discussion, and since that tied him up, he couldn't give me a hint of what was going on.

I watched my parents go to the check-in desk together and begin talking with the woman at the counter, with Fred listening in. I followed behind them, still carrying a suitcase. I prepared to hoist the suitcase to the counter for baggage check-in when suddenly, inexplicably, I saw my father turn from the desk, pick up his suitcase, and walk briskly toward the door. My mother picked up her suitcase and took off behind him, followed by Fred with the other suitcase.

For a split second I was unable to react. I knew my parents had to be in Chicago within forty-eight hours to pick up their Hawaii tour. I had no idea why everyone was suddenly grabbing bags and rushing back in the direction of the parking lot.

It was just the sort of situation I always seemed to face with my family; everybody forgot that I might want to know what was happening and not be just a mindless groupie. It wasn't even dawn, and I had given up good sleep on a weekend to help, so I felt that I deserved some explanation. I was totally teed off. I took off after the three retreating backs, and as I approached them, I blew up. "Would somebody like to tell me just what is going on?" I asked in an icy voice.

I found out that due to a strike there were no seats on any planes to Chicago, so my parents had immediately decided to get back to their car, gas up, and drive there instead. Long after my parents had left, I was still thinking about what had happened, how terrible it had made me feel, and how I wanted to find a way to keep things like that from happening again.

All the words I had been writing, all the anger I had poured out on paper, hadn't done me much good. I still wasn't finished. Only honesty with my family would help.

I was grateful that I had begun to build a relationship with Randy. Over the next few months, I experienced something I had craved for my entire adult life—the chance to talk honestly with a member of my family. Randy told me up front how much he cared about me, and that made the rest easy. His wife, Judy, watched their two children for the weekend so that Randy and I could have two days alone at the cabin.

These were days of unbelievable intensity. We got to know each other again as individuals, and we were amazed at how growing up under similar circumstances had influenced what we'd become. We were more alike than we'd realized. Randy told me that he felt as though I had suddenly handed him more pieces to a puzzle. I felt exactly the same way.

My growing friendship with my brother helped me find the strength to do the one thing I'd always feared: risk losing my family's love. I started by writing a letter.

Dear Family:

My book is back for revisions. It's a paper Godzilla that refuses to die. I've never been satisfied with it because I couldn't shake the feeling that it needs a tidy wrap up.

An important element has been missing. It took me a while to realize that I'll never be finished with this book until I write a final chapter. This is it—my letter to you.

I knew from the outset that for another book about deafness to be of any value, it had to be totally honest. This meant that I would have to write about myself because my experiences with deafness are the ones I know best. But I would sooner walk barefoot across a sea of broken glass then dredge up memories of some of my experiences. Writing this book was by far the hardest work I've ever done.

I started writing after attending the Deaf Way conference, out of a deep feeling of obligation to many wonderful deaf persons I met. Over and over I heard them say that the world never fully understands deafness because deaf people do not write books. They pointed out that in any library, most of the books about deafness are written by hearing persons.

I loved the conference and its celebration of Deaf culture, but it was a painful reminder of my alienation from both the hearing world and Deaf world. I'm not unique in feeling this alienation. I have met hundreds of people who feel the same way. We're a scattered army of souls looking for a place to belong.

When we can't function in the world that requires hearing to communicate, there is no automatic membership in the world where vision replaces hearing. Like many other deaf persons, I tried to cling to the world in which I was once comfortable, but the hearing world is one that has been often unwilling to adapt to my needs. You're part of that world.

Since I moved to Reston three years ago, I've been watching a man who lives in a neighboring county. His name wouldn't ring a bell with you, but he's been famous both in these parts and nationally. For years, he was a spokesman for the Oral Deaf Adults Section of the A. G. Bell Association. He's a successful, highly intelligent, extremely literate man, and he is indirectly responsible for screwing up an entire generation of deaf kids, including me.

This man has had lots of exposure while telling teachers and parents and deaf people that sign language is a worthless crutch. He urged deaf persons to follow his example and learn to speak and read lips with ease. We tried to stick to his recommendations, sacrificing true communication in our attempts to become like him. He was so adamant about the rightness of his cause that sometimes he'd make a scene if a sign language interpreter was present at a meeting. He said that the hand movements of signers distracted him when he was trying to focus on the faces of speakers.

Now, in his later years, his man has surprised me by using signs himself. He's showing up at meetings and mixing with deaf sign language users, the people he once disdained as Bart Simpson-variety underachievers. I hope he's finding out what I began to learn fifteen years ago.

You're probably wondering what this fellow has to do with much of anything. The answer is that he's a monument to the life I am trying to be free of. I've been experiencing a metamorphosis. As I write this letter, I seek to complete it.

My editor read a draft of my book and remarked that I came across a person with a great deal of anger. She's right. For a long time I fooled myself into thinking that anger didn't have to be negative. I used my anger as the source of my motivation. I wanted to do what I could to make sure no one else would have to experience the things that had hurt me. Slowly, I have come to trust myself and know that I can let go of the anger without losing my driving force.

I have shared some of my thoughts with Randy, after a misunderstanding last year helped us become more open with one another. He's made me realize that I have to find the courage to continue to be honest, not just with him, but with all of you.

I'm having a hard time doing that. It seems that when I want to say something important, it comes out bearing little resemblance to what I meant. Speaking is, for me, an act requiring great concentration. Because I don't have the reinforcement of hearing my words, as you do, I have to pay attention to how I form each sound when I speak. Sometimes I'm trying so hard to make my words understood by your ears that I can't make my message understood by your brains. It won't surprise you to know that many people say I come across better on paper. That's why I chose to write what is so crucial to me.

I have a confession to make. One of the greatest mistakes I've made over the years is to become the Cheryl Streep of the family. I've been play-acting to be the kind of person that I thought you'd be proud of and comfortable with. I have tried to hide from you much of my confusion, frustration, and pain.

The truth is that it has often been hard for me to be around you. I want more than anything to feel like I am part of our family. But because I can't be involved in the routine exchange of family chatter, I usually feel like Fred is your blood kin and I am the in-law.

The sides of me that you've been seeing in recent years may have seemed jarringly inconsistent, but actually they're the first glimpses I've allowed of myself. You'll be seeing more of that person and not the Great Impostor.

Working with other deaf and hard of hearing persons has been my private hell. Just like many preachers and psychiatrists, I'm great at helping other people solve their problems and inept at getting my own house in order. I've counseled a lot of people and their families on how to be more sensitive to each other's needs and told them what not to do. I learned all these things from the mistakes we've made with each other. It hasn't been a great way to live.

In the years after I lost my hearing, I rarely told you what I was learning about deafness and about myself. Marriage to Fred has already taught me the folly of expecting those close to me to be clairvoyant. So let me begin explaining some of what I've discovered.

It wasn't until I learned my first signs at age twenty-five that I began to understand how much I had been missing. People have always been amazed by my speechreading skills, and I've never met a person who surpasses me at guessing mouth movements, unless that person had a great deal more hearing. Even with peak conditions: good lighting, high energy level, and a person who articulates well, I'm still guessing at half of what I see on the lips. You wouldn't know that unless you questioned me closely. I'm a great mimic, and I have been superb at the art of self-delusion. I made a good actor because I convinced *myself* that I understood everything. Just like the way I watched movies I didn't understand and made up the plot in my head, I invented stories about our lives. It was hard at times to separate the real from the fantasy.

We never got into the habit of using a pencil and paper in our house. When I couldn't understand things that you were saying, I had to learn to live with unknowns. "Never mind" and "forget it" were routine in many of my conversations with you. I recently watched Dr. Sam Trychin at a meeting of a Self Help for Hard of Hearing People chapter. One of the participants told Dr. Trychin how much she hated asking someone to repeat a statement only to be told "it's not important." Dr. Trychin pointed out that the reason these words are hurtful is that they imply *"you're* not important." And that's how I felt when you said them.

Speechreading is EXHAUSTING. I hate having to depend on it. Once I had experienced the kind of freedom sign language could give me, it became harder and harder to go back to struggling without it. When I'm around people who don't sign, I feel like someone with a perfectly good pair of legs who's been told to crawl everywhere.

Gayle, when you started to learn signs and fingerspelling, I was so happy! I watched your girls play games with fingerspelling and knew I could hope for a better future. I love the way Judy has tried to remember the fingerspelling she learned long ago, helping me out of tight spots. Now Mom and Dad are also taking a class! I know that it's slow going, but it means so much that you care enough to try.

I deeply appreciate all the small ways you've tried to include me. When you boycott television shows without captions during my visits, I feel honored.

Lots of times when I've been with you, I manipulate to pull you aside, sometimes with Fred's collusion. This is my chance to catch up on your lives. We don't get many opportunities for that, though. Sometimes you're too busy, restless, or not feeling particularly talkative. And lots of times someone else will decide to join us. When that happens, I quickly become the odd one out. It's so hard to speechread more than one person at a time that I look for an excuse to exit the conversation.

On our long drives home, Fred tells me what he's learned from being around all of you. He seems to pick up a lot for a guy who spends so much time playing video games or watching television. You probably don't even realize how much information I miss, but Fred knows because he has to endure my questions.

Sometimes you use Fred as a channel to me, because it's easier. At long last, let me warn you that the words "tell Cheryl" create a chemical reaction in Fred's body. The result is instant amnesia. Fred is human, and using him is like playing "gossip." A lot can get lost in the translation.

Writing my book has helped me figure out why I became the person I am. What it couldn't do was what I needed most, to put a stop to my acting. I have a double life. The Cheryl that you see is very different from the one that my friends and co-workers know.

I have titled my book "Life as a Spectator Sport" [now *Seeds of Disquiet*]. I want to close this letter, my final chapter, and start anew as a participant in all possible parts of my life.

When you guys are all laughing at a punch line I didn't catch, I won't be the fake who tries to be "one of the gang" by laughing along. I would love to be a partner in your conversations, but if that's not possible I can still enjoy watching you enjoy yourselves. If I get bored, I'm going to start the dishes, play with Katie, or sneak a peek at Randy's folder to read his latest works.

I'm no longer going to let myself feel like the family party pooper. I used to waste a lot of time doing the things that I thought would make you happy but that made me miserable. Don't feel bad about wanting to do something I can't enjoy. It's not YOUR fault that I'm deaf, any more than it's mine. Have a good time. Remember that I've always been a resourceful person and I'm good at keeping myself amused.

My nieces are all neat kids and I'll happily stay with them so you can go out. You do trust Weird Aunt Cheryl with them, don't you? My slate is clear of pyro-, klepto- and other manias.

Please don't push me to go to the movies with you. When I was younger, there were a few I wanted to see out of curiosity. Now that I've used a caption decoder, movie theaters only make me more conscious of what I'm missing. Sure, I'd like to see movies on the big screen as you do, with bass booming through my seat. You can help by putting your rear ends in motion and working with me to get captions in theaters. It's not just for me. If you live long enough, you'll need them too.

When you go in the living room to talk with only dim light from the corners, I won't be sitting with you, trying hard to look interested in whatever you're discussing. And most important, when I don't understand you, I won't try to bluff. You can try rewording your sentence, fingerspell it, write it down, or walk away. It's your choice. I expect you to give me the same consideration when you listen to my imperfect speech.

I don't need your approval, but I do need your love. Then again, who am I kidding? The approval would be nice.

And so I have resolved henceforth to be . . . Cheryl Ann McIntosh Heppner, not Cheryl Streep. I think we're a neat family and I'm glad I grew up learning a strong sense of values with people who kicked my butt when I deserved it. That tough rear end has proved to be an asset in many situations.

Love,

Cheryl

——————30——

Many things are changing. While I was crafting my letter of confession, I learned that my parents were taking their first class in sign language.

After thirty-three years as a deaf person, there is still plenty of room for memorable firsts. Seated in a busy restaurant with Mom, Fred, and the Woodhouses, I had the indescribable experience of sharing a private joke—in sign language—with my father.

Too many other things stay the same. The deaf and hard of hearing people who share their lives with me at the Resource Center still don't have enough services, and I still don't have enough time. I don't know if I'll ever be able to accept that there's only so much that can be crammed into twenty-four hours each day. Patience was never one of my virtues. I like the epitaph Robert Frost chose: "I would have written of me on my stone: I had a lover's quarrel with the world." I plan to be cremated, so I invest in people as a permanent epitaph. Their dreams are mine.

While writing this book, I was surprised to find out that I am not a bad person. I always felt that I somehow lacked key ingredients and therefore suffered from gaping character flaws. During the past two years I've taken personality tests that seemed to confirm it. The results used all these words that sounded negative, but true—suspicious, restless, stubborn, questioning authority, causing action, good at managing trouble. Fortunately, I'm still going to the cabin for weekends, and during my stretches of quiet reflection I've figured out that without these traits I never would have done anything positive.

What a relief it was to find out I could stop carrying the baggage of being born bad! It's amazing how easily a kid's head can get messed up without anybody realizing it. The disparaging remarks I heard at a very young age, made by people who compared me to my sister, had always stayed with me, my personal albatross. They got heavy reinforcement after I became deaf and everyone who failed to communicate with me walked away with facial expressions I read as disgust. How was I supposed to know that they weren't always disgusted with me? Later I compounded the mistake by continuing to compare myself with other people and always coming up short. I could never find peace with myself.

I'm beginning to find it now.

One of my sign language students, Lessa Schwenk, gave me a copy of the Rutgers Creed. At this point in my life I feel it is an utterly perfect set of rules to live by, and it is a fitting closing for my book.

The Rutgers Creed

I make this pledge
which I shall keep
at every age
in every circumstance
despite anger
in the face of fear
to my sisters and brothers
whether they resemble me or not
please me or not
love me or not
I will, in every act of life
cherish human rights
seek reconciliation
and give love.